MARIKA HANBURY TENISON

Recipes from a Country Kitchen

Illustrated by Stephen Forster

HART-DAVIS, MACGIBBON
GRANADA PUBLISHING

Published by Granada Publishing in
Hart-Davis, MacGibbon Ltd 1978

Granada Publishing Limited
Frogmore, St Albans, Herts AL2 2NF
and
3 Upper James Street, London W1R 4BP
1221 Avenue of the Americas, New York, NY 10020, USA
117 York Street, Sydney, NSW 2000, Australia
100 Skyway Avenue, Toronto, Ontario, Canada M9W 3A6
Trio City, Coventry Street, Johannesburg 2001, South Africa
CML Centre, Queen & Wyndham, Auckland 1, New Zealand

ISBN 0 246 10968 8

Printed in Great Britain by
Richard Clay (The Chaucer Press) Ltd
Bungay, Suffolk

Recipes from a Country Kitchen

Contents

Foreword

Those who don't know the West of England might tend to dismiss its cuisine as cream teas, cider and Cheddar cheese. In reality traditional West Country cooking has a richness almost unsurpassed in the rest of the British Isles. It is well worth knowing; the variety and downright wholesome good sense of West Country cooking makes it attractive to any cook, especially one with a hungry family to feed, and the fresh country taste of the dishes makes them a refreshing joy in these days of substitute, frozen and convenience foods.

To start with, the West Country has access to a larger variety of fresh, natural ingredients than any other part of our islands. Almost at their doorsteps most West Country-women have the rich bounty of the sea, with an almost mind-boggling superabundance of shellfish, flat and deep sea fish, both known and little known. Mackerel come into the harbours by the ton; dabs and megrim make, to my mind, just as good eating as sole, their expensive relative; red gurnards goggle from fishmongers' slabs, skate wings glisten white as snow and the tender-fleshed John Dory can be found throughout the summer. Hens (small clams), cockles and mussels can be gathered from the sea shore; queens (baby scallops) are lifted from the ocean bed and oysters multiply in the warmth and shelter of the Helford estuary. Crabs are large and succulent, lobsters sweet and tender and even the pinky prawn can be had for a bit of patience, wet ankles and a shrimping net. Rivers, and now reservoirs, boast salmon as large as any caught on the Tay and plump brown trout of indefinably delicate flavour.

On the farms inland rich soil and succulent grass feed cattle, sheep and pigs. There is game in the woods, wild fruit in the hedgerows, mushrooms to be picked in the fields and, in the market gardens, vegetables of all kinds are grown for the London markets.

From the Phoenicians the West Country learnt the use of
saffron and clotted (or clouted) cream, and from Brittany
Cornwall retains the secret of dishes with a Celtic origin.
From its travellers and explorers the West has learnt and
made good use of the spices and exotic ingredients of other
parts of the world, so that even the most humble West
Country food has a flair and flavour all its own.

I have lived in and out of the West Country all my life. As
a child I spent my holidays and as many weekends as I could
in Devon and Somerset. When I married I moved to Cornwall for good, my home is there and my happiness too.

In this book are recipes I have been collecting since I was
eleven and first discovered cookery; dishes I have learnt
about from countrywomen during the last year; ideas from
old manuscripts; and the memories of the grandparents of
those who have lived their lives in the West of England.

The food is food for everyone and every occasion. Much
of it is simple, all of it is good and some dishes are grand
enough to set before the Queen herself. West Country food,
to my mind, is *real* food and that, these days, can only be
a joy and satisfaction.

May you enjoy it as much as I and my family do.

MARIKA HANBURY TENISON
Maidenwell, Cornwall.
August 1977

Metric Weights and Measures

g = gram; kg = kilogram; ml = millilitre

EXACT EQUIVALENTS	APPROXIMATE EQUIVALENTS	METRIC COOKERY
	$\frac{1}{2}$ oz = 15 g	
1 oz = 28·3 g	1 oz = 30 g	1 oz = 25 g
4 oz = 113·4 g	4 oz = 120 g	4 oz = 100 g
8 oz = 226·8 g	8 oz = 240 g	8 oz = 225 g
1 lb = 453·6 g	1 lb = 480 g	1 lb = 450 g
2·2 lb = 1 kg	$2\frac{1}{4}$ lb = 1 kg	2–$2\frac{1}{4}$ lb = 1 kg
	$\frac{1}{8}$ pt ($2\frac{1}{2}$ fl oz) = 75 ml	
$\frac{1}{4}$ pt = 142 ml	$\frac{1}{4}$ pt (5 fl oz) = 150 ml	$\frac{1}{4}$ pt = 125–150 ml
$\frac{1}{2}$ pt = 284 ml	$\frac{1}{2}$ pt (10 fl oz) = 275 ml	$\frac{1}{2}$ pt = 250–275 ml
$\frac{3}{4}$ pt = 426 ml	$\frac{3}{4}$ pt (15 fl oz) = 425 ml	$\frac{3}{4}$ pt = 400–425 ml
1 pt = 568 ml	1 pt (20 fl oz) = 575 ml	1 pt = 500–575 ml
$1\frac{3}{4}$ pt = 0·994 litre	$1\frac{3}{4}$ pt (35 fl oz) = 1 litre	$1\frac{3}{4}$ pt = 900 ml

Note: the left-hand column is purely for reference. The centre column is for doing quick conversions; the equivalents are accurate enough for practical cookery purposes, as grams and millilitres are so small that plus or minus five makes very little difference. The right-hand column shows the amounts generally used in metric cookery, where 25 g is used instead of 1 oz, and 25 ml instead of 1 fl oz. This produces a dish which is slightly smaller, but still has the correct proportion of solids to liquids.

Oven Temperatures

DESCRIPTION	ELECTRIC SETTING		GAS MARK
	°Fahrenheit	°Centigrade	Regulo
very slow	225	110	$\frac{1}{4}$
very slow	250	130	$\frac{1}{2}$
slow	275	140	1
slow	300	150	2
very moderate	325	160	3
moderate	350	180	4
moderate to	375	190	5
moderately hot	400	200	6
hot	425	220	7
hot	450	230	8
very hot	475	240	9

1

Soups for Warmth and Goodness

Steaming tureens of aromatic broths and soups, full of nutrition and flavour and made from the best of country-fresh ingredients, herbs and subtle seasonings.

HOME-GROWN vegetables, hedgerow herbs and the fruits of the sea all form the base of many delicious soups, with the final touch often being given by a generous measure of finely-chopped parsley from the garden. This is a field when the cook can let her artistry and imagination run riot, and some of the best soups we have ever had at Maidenwell have been made up of an often extraordinary concoction of miscellaneous items which were all I had to hand.

Soup making, on the whole, is fairly straightforward. A stock pot, made from raw or cooked meat, poultry, fish or bones, vegetable trimmings and herbs is a great asset. But should you not have one on the boil there are good stock cubes these days which, providing they are not used to excess, can be useful as a background flavouring. It is worth while keeping tomato skins, onion skins, mushroom peeling, celery leaves and other vegetables that are not too strong in flavour to boil up and use as flavouring ingredients for soups based on commercial stock cubes.

For extra nourishment and texture soups can be thickened with a little flour, smoothed to a paste with a knob of softened butter and beaten in before serving. Or beat a couple of egg yolks until smooth, blend with a little of the hot liquid or with cream and add to the soup before serving; never allow to boil.

Soup must be served really piping hot, so always heat the bowls it is to be served in – nothing is more depressing than lukewarm soup.

Soups can be one of the most inexpensive ways of starting a meal and, for children and adults alike, one of the most pleasant and comforting delights, especially on a cold winter day.

THE USE OF HERBS AND SPICES

The use of fresh herbs and spices has always been an integral part of West Country cooking. Many herbs once grew wild and were later cultivated in country gardens, and you still see the remnants of a sizable herb patch in the gardens of even the smallest country cottages. Marigold petals, thyme, sage, marjoram and savory all played their part in traditional dishes, and parsley, above all, was used with a lavishness that today's cooks would find surprising. Cooks often had to make do with very little, and they often relied on a mixture of herbs and spices to provide the flavour that was lacking in other ingredients.

Many of these herb gardens disappeared during the last World War, but they are slowly coming back, and the use of fresh herbs in cooking is now fairly widespread, but if you don't have access to them yourself, there are some really good dried and freeze-dried herbs on the market. Dried herbs have had their essential oils concentrated in the drying process, and should be used with a lighter hand than the fresh ingredients. As a rough guide, 2 sprigs of any fresh herb (with the exception of parsley) is equivalent to about $\frac{1}{8}$ teaspoon of a good dried product. Soften dried herbs in a little warm water or lemon juice before using them to bring out their flavour and aroma.

Of the spices used in the West Country, saffron is by far the most important. This was brought into the country by the Phoenicians and has played a major role in cooking in Cornwall and, to a certain extent, Devon ever since.

Saffron is an expensive spice (the yellow strands are gathered from the autumn crocus and you need a lot of strands), but you only need a little to provide the flavour required. The saffron is usually sold in strand form, and can be bought from supermarkets or chemists in small sachets.

Crab Soup

Soup made from the brown and white meat is rich and should be followed by a light main course.

Serves 6

Pinch saffron
1 tablespoon boiling water

1 small onion
1½ oz (40 g) butter
2 tablespoons flour
1½ pints (875 ml) milk
½ lb (225 g) crab meat (equal amounts brown and white)
Salt and freshly-ground black pepper
Pinch nutmeg
1½ pints (875 ml) chicken stock
½ teaspoon anchovy essence or 1 anchovy fillet (mashed
 to a paste)
3 tablespoons double cream
2 tablespoons sherry

Soak the saffron in the boiling water for 15 minutes. Peel and very finely chop the onion. Melt the butter, add the onion and cook over a low heat until soft and transparent. Add the flour and mix well. Gradually add the milk, stirring continually over a medium high heat until the liquid comes to the boil and is thickened and smooth. Add the brown crab meat and season with salt, pepper and a pinch of nutmeg. Simmer for three minutes.

Strain the saffron liquid and add it to the soup base with the chicken stock, bring to the boil and simmer for a further 5 minutes. Rub the soup through a fine sieve and return it to a clean pan. Heat through, add the anchovy, cream, sherry and white crab meat, check seasoning. Heat through without boiling and serve at once.

Cockle or Queen Soup

Serves 4

1 medium onion
2 leeks
1 oz (25 g) butter
1 tablespoon flour
1½ pints (875 ml) chicken stock
½ pint (275 ml) milk

Salt and freshly-ground pepper
2 bay leaves
3 tablespoons boiling water
½ teaspoon strand saffron
8 oz (225 g) cockles or queens
2 tablespoons finely-chopped parsley
1 tablespoon finely-chopped chives
4 tablespoons double cream

Peel and finely chop the onion. Wash and thinly slice the leeks. Melt the butter in a large heavy pan. Add the onion and leeks and cook over a low heat until soft and transparent. Add the flour and mix well. Gradually add the stock and milk, stirring continually over a medium high heat until thick and smooth. Bring to the boil, season with salt and pepper, add the bay leaves and simmer for 15 minutes.

Pour the boiling water over the saffron and leave for 5 minutes. Strain the liquid and add it to the soup. Continue to simmer for a further 5 minutes, then remove the bay leaves.

If queens are used, cut into small pieces. Add the cockles or queens to the soup with the parsley, chives and cream. Check seasoning, heat through and serve.

Cream of Potato Soup with Scallops

Serves 4

1 large onion
½ lb (225 g) potatoes
1 oz (25 g) butter
1½ pints (875 ml) chicken stock
Salt and freshly-ground black pepper
4 scallops
1 pint (575 ml) milk
1 egg yolk
3 tablespoons double cream
2 tablespoons finely-chopped parsley

Peel and finely chop the onion. Peel the potatoes and cut into small dice. Melt the butter in a heavy saucepan. Add the onion and potatoes and cook over a low heat until the fat has been absorbed and the onion is transparent. Pour over the stock, mix well, bring to the boil, season with salt and pepper and simmer until the vegetables are tender.

Purée the vegetables through a sieve, a food mill or in a liquidiser and return to a clean pan.

Remove the red coral part of the scallops and pull off any black intestine. Heat the milk in a saucepan, add the white part of the scallops and poach for 3 minutes. Remove scallops with a slotted spoon and cut into small dice. Slice the red coral of the scallops.

Beat the egg, gradually add the milk the scallops were cooked in and the cream. Add this mixture to the vegetable purée and heat gently, without boiling, for about 3 minutes, stirring all the time. Add the white and pink parts of the scallops, check seasoning, heat through and serve at once with the parsley scattered over the top.

Mackerel Soup

Far more than a soup, in fact a main course that is beautifully aromatic and extremely satisfying.

Serves 6

4 small mackerel
Salt and freshly-ground black pepper
Flour
1 large potato
2 leeks
1 clove garlic
1 teaspoon saffron
1 teaspoon boiling water
1 oz (25 g) butter
1 tin of tomatoes 14 oz (396 g)
2 bay leaves

1½ pints (875 ml) chicken stock
½ lb (225 g) cockles
Parsley and chives
4 slices French bread
Olive oil or lard for frying

Remove the heads and tails from the mackerel and clean the fish. Cut the fish in 1 in (2½ cm) thick slices and coat the pieces in seasoned flour.

Peel the potato and cut into small dice. Clean and slice the leeks. Peel and finely chop the garlic. Soak the saffron in two tablespoons of boiling water for five minutes and then strain the liquid.

Melt the butter in a large heavy pan. Add the potato, garlic and leeks and cook over a low heat, shaking the pan to prevent sticking, until the potato is transparent and the fat has been absorbed. Add the fish and cook over a medium high heat for 3 minutes, turning the fish every now and then until the slices are lightly browned. Add the tomatoes, broken up with a fork, and the bay leaves and simmer for 10 minutes. Blend in the stock, add the cockles and saffron water, season with salt and pepper and simmer for a further 5 minutes. Remove bay leaves. Mix in the parsley and chives.

Fry the bread until crisp and golden brown in olive oil or lard. Drain on kitchen paper and float a piece of fried bread on the top of each filled soup bowl.

Eel Soup

Serves 6

1 lb (450 g) small eels
1 small onion
1½ oz (40 g) butter
2 tablespoons flour
2½ pints (1¼ litres) fish or chicken stock
Bouquet garni made of a sprig of parsley, thyme, sage, marjoram and 2 bay leaves tied together

    Salt, freshly-ground black pepper and a pinch mace
    5 tablespoons double or soured cream
    4 tablespoons very finely-chopped parsley

Ask your fishmonger to clean and skin the eels. Cut them into 1-in (2½-cm) long pieces. Peel and very finely chop the onion. Melt the butter in a heavy pan. Add the onion and cook over a very low heat, stirring to prevent browning, until the onion is soft and transparent. Remove the onion with a slotted spoon and add the eels to the juices in the pan. Continue to cook over a low heat for 5 minutes without browning. Remove the eels with a slotted spoon and mix the flour into the juices in the pan.

Add the stock, stirring continually over a high heat until the soup base is thickened and smooth. Add the onion, eels and bouquet garni, season with salt, pepper and mace, bring to the boil and simmer for 20 minutes or until the eels are tender and their flesh comes easily away from the bones.

Remove the bouquet garni, lift out the eels on a slotted spoon and separate the bones from the flesh. Return the eel flesh to the soup, mix in the cream, check seasoning and heat through without boiling. Stir in the parsley just before serving the soup.

Country Mushroom Soup

Chopped chives stirred in at the last minute add enormously to the flavour.

Serves 4

    4 oz (125 g) firm button mushrooms
    1 small onion
    1 oz (25 g) butter
    2 teaspoons cornflour
    2 pints (1 litre) chicken stock (or water and stock cubes)
    Salt and freshly-ground black pepper
    Pinch of nutmeg

2 tablespoons sherry
2½ fl oz (75 ml) cream
2 tablespoons finely-chopped chives

Pick over the mushrooms but don't wash them unless absolutely necessary. Finely chop the mushrooms with their stalks. Peel and finely chop the onion.

Melt the butter, add the onion and cook over a low heat until the onion is soft and transparent. Add the mushrooms and cook slowly for 3 minutes, stirring every now and then to prevent sticking. Sprinkle over the cornflour, mix well and gradually blend in the stock, stirring continually over a medium high heat until the soup comes to the boil and is smooth. Season with salt, pepper and a pinch of nutmeg and simmer gently for 15–20 minutes.

Purée the soup through a food mill, a sieve or in a liquidiser, return to a clean pan. Blend in the sherry and cream, check seasoning and heat through without boiling. Stir in chives just before serving.

Somerset Celery Soup

Serves 4

2 small heads celery
1 large onion
1½ pints (875 ml) chicken stock (or water and 2 chicken stock cubes)
1 egg yolk
¼ pint (150 ml) single cream
Salt and freshly-ground black pepper
Pinch mace
Pinch sugar

Wash the celery and remove the leaves, reserving one or two for garnish. Chop stalks into 1-in (2½-cm) pieces. Peel and roughly chop the onion. Add the celery and onion to a saucepan of fast-boiling salted water and boil until tender.

Drain well and purée the vegetables through a sieve, a food mill or in a liquidiser.

Combine the celery and onion purée with the stock, bring to the boil and simmer for 5 minutes.

Beat the egg yolk with the cream, add a little of the soup, beat until smooth and then add the cream mixture to the rest of the soup. Stir until the soup is smooth – do not boil. Season with salt, pepper, a little mace and a pinch of sugar and serve with a garnish of very finely-chopped celery leaves.

Fresh Pea Soup

Useful to make with any peas that have just gone a little over their prime. The added pea pods provide extra flavour.

Serves 6

1 lb (450 g) peas
2 pints (1 litre) chicken stock
4 sprigs mint
3 sprigs parsley
½ pint (275 ml) single cream
2 teaspoons flour
Salt and freshly-ground black pepper
Croûtons of fried bread

Shell the peas and reserve half the pods. Bring the stock to the boil and add the peas, reserved pea pods, the mint and parsley. Return to the boil and cook until peas and pods are tender. Rub the soup through a fine sieve or through a food mill (do not use a liquidiser as this would make the soup too thick and leave in the fibres of the pods). Return the soup to a clean pan.

Combine a little of the cream with the flour and mix until smooth. Blend in the remaining cream and add to the soup. Cook over a low heat, without boiling, until the soup has thickened a little. Season with salt and pepper and serve with the crisply-fried croûtons.

Likky Soup

A soup found in many parts of England and a good warmer for a cold winter evening.

Serves 6

4 young leeks
1 onion
2 rashers streaky bacon
3 large potatoes
$\frac{1}{2}$ oz (15 g) butter
2 pints (1 litre) water or chicken stock
Salt and freshly-ground black pepper
1 pint (575 ml) milk
A knob of butter
1 tablespoon finely-chopped parsley

Clean and roughly chop the leeks and onion. Remove and reserve the rinds from the bacon and finely chop the rashers. Peel the potatoes and cut them into small dice.

Cook the bacon and rinds in a large heavy pan, over a low heat, until the fat has melted. Remove the rinds, add the butter, leeks and onion and continue to cook over a low heat until the vegetables are soft and transparent and the fats have been absorbed. Add the potatoes, pour over the water or stock and season with salt and pepper. Bring to the boil and simmer for about 20 minutes or until potatoes are soft.

Add the milk and a knob of butter the size of a walnut, heat through, check seasoning and stir in the parsley just before serving.

Cream of Cauliflower Soup

Although this soup is basically smooth it has a pleasant crunchy texture of small bits of cauliflower which transforms it from the bland consistency the soup usually has into something really delicious.

Serves 6

1 large cauliflower
1¾ pints (900 ml) chicken stock
Salt, pepper and a pinch of nutmeg
2 egg yolks
¼ pint (150 ml) single cream
½ pint (275 ml) milk
Croûtons of fried bread

Remove the green leaves of the cauliflower and the tough end of the stalk and divide into florets. Cook the cauliflower until tender in a little boiling salted water. Drain well. Reserve about three of the florets and purée the remainder of the cauliflower through a fine sieve, a food mill or in a liquidiser.

Pour the puréed cauliflower into a saucepan, add the stock and mix well. Bring slowly to the boil over a low heat and season with salt and pepper. Simmer for 10 minutes.

Beat the egg yolks with the cream. Chop the reserved cauliflower florets. Add the egg mixture and the milk to the soup and cook over a low heat, without boiling, until the soup is thickened and satiny. Add the chopped cauliflower and serve with crisp croûtons of fried bread.

Lovage Soup

The taste, some say, is of summer herbs; to others it has a faint curry flavour that reminds them of the East; to me it is the gentle, bitter-sweet aroma of lovage from the garden that comes to mind as I take the first sip.

Serves 6

Large bunch lovage leaves and stalks 3 oz (75 g)
1 lb (450 g) potatoes
2 onions
1 oz (25 g) butter

1 pint (575 ml) chicken stock (or water and 1 chicken
stock cube)
1 pint (575 ml) milk
Salt and freshly-ground black pepper
Pinch nutmeg
$\frac{1}{4}$ pint (150 ml) double cream

Roughly chop the lovage leaves (reserving two for garnish);
peel the potatoes and cut into small dice. Peel and finely chop
the onions.

Melt the butter in a heavy saucepan. Add the onion and
potato and cook over a low heat, without browning until the
onion is soft and transparent and the butter has been
absorbed. Add the lovage and cook for a further 2 minutes.

Pour in the stock and milk, bring to the boil and season
with salt, pepper and a pinch of nutmeg. Cover and simmer
gently for 20 minutes or until potatoes are soft.

Purée the soup through a food mill, a sieve or in a
liquidiser and return to a clean pan. Blend in the cream,
check seasoning and heat through without boiling if the soup
is to be served hot. Chill in a refrigerator until icy cold to
serve on a summer evening.

Garnish with finely-chopped fresh lovage leaves.

Potato Soup

This is really a cold weather, winter soup, but with the
addition of some yoghurt and some additional chopped
chives it also makes a very good cold soup to serve at the end
of the summer when the old potatoes are well into their
stride.

Serves 6

3 large potatoes
2 large onions
2 cloves garlic
$1\frac{1}{2}$ oz (40 g) butter

2 bay leaves
Pinch finely-chopped marjoram and thyme
$\frac{3}{4}$ pint (425 ml) milk
1 pint (575 ml) chicken stock
Salt and freshly-ground black pepper
Pinch nutmeg
3 tablespoons single cream
1 tablespoon finely-chopped chives

Peel and dice the potatoes. Peel and chop the onions. Peel and finely chop the garlic cloves. Melt the butter in a large heavy pan. Add the potatoes, onions, garlic cloves, bay leaves, marjoram and thyme and cook over a low heat until the onions are transparent and all the butter has been absorbed.

Add the milk and stock, mix well and cook over a medium high heat until the vegetables are tender. Remove the bay leaves, purée the soup through a sieve or food mill and return it to a clean pan. Season with salt and freshly-ground black pepper and a pinch of nutmeg. Heat through and mix in the cream and chopped chives.

To serve cold: Cool the soup, stir in $\frac{1}{4}$ pint of yoghurt or soured cream and mix in an additional spoonful of chopped chives.

Split Pea Soup

Make this soup when you are having a boiled bacon or ham dish and use the stock to flavour the soup.

Serves 6–8

1 lb (450 g) split peas
2 onions
2 carrots
3 sticks celery
3 pints (1$\frac{1}{2}$ litres) ham stock
$\frac{1}{2}$ teaspoon sugar

Freshly-ground black pepper
1 oz (25 g) butter
1 oz (25 g) flour
3 slices white bread
Bacon fat
1 tablespoon very finely-chopped mint

Cover the peas with cold water to which a pinch of bi-carbonate of soda has been added and leave in a cool place for 24 hours.

Peel and roughly chop the onions and carrots. Chop the celery. Drain the peas well and put in a large pan with the stock. Bring to the boil, remove any scum from the surface and add the vegetables. Add the sugar and season with pepper, return to the boil and simmer for about 1 hour or until the peas are tender.

Purée the soup through a sieve, a food mill or in a liquidiser.

Melt the butter in a clean pan. Add the flour and mix well. Gradually blend in the puréed soup, stirring continually until the soup is thick and smooth and comes to the boil.

Remove the crusts from the bread and cut it into small dice. Fry the croûtons of bread in bacon fat until crisp and golden brown. Serve the soup with the croûtons of bread and a little chopped mint floating on the surface of each serving.

Spinach and Turnip Soup

The spinach and turnip combination is a good one. Those who don't admit to liking turnip will fail to recognise it, but the root adds flavour and richness to the soup.

Serves 4–5

12 oz (350 g) spinach
1 medium turnip
1 large onion

1 medium carrot
3 sticks celery
½ oz (15 g) butter
2 sprigs parsley
1 small sprig thyme
2 pints (1 litre) light chicken stock or (water and 2 chicken stock cubes)
Salt and freshly-ground black pepper
½ oz (15 g) butter
½ oz (15 g) flour

Wash the spinach and squeeze excess water out well. Peel and dice the turnip. Peel and roughly chop the onion and carrot. Clean and chop the celery. Melt the butter in a heavy pan. Add the vegetables and herbs and cook over a low heat until the vegetables are soft. Add the stock, bring to the boil, season with salt and pepper and simmer for about 20 minutes or until the vegetables are quite tender.

Purée the soup through a sieve, a food mill or in a liquidiser and return to a clean pan.

Mix together the butter and the flour until smooth. Add this to the soup and mix with a wire whisk until the soup is smooth and slightly thickened. Check for seasoning before serving.

Note: The soup can be served with small croûtons of crisply-fried bread or with small suet dumplings (see page 110).

Chicken and Barley Soup

When you need reviving and extra strength, a nourishing soup gives more instant strength than a double whisky or a rum and shrub. After a hard day's work (or night's work) a soup like this brings almost instant vitality.

Serves 6

3 oz (75 g) pearl barley
2 lb (900 g) leeks
1 oz (25 g) chicken or bacon fat or butter
2½ pints (1¼ litres) chicken stock
2 bay leaves
Salt and freshly-ground black pepper
8 oz (225 g) cooked chicken
¼ pint (150 ml) milk
1 small bunch watercress
¼ pint (150 ml) single cream

Cook the barley in boiling, salted water for about 1 hour until soft, drain well and rinse in cold water.

Clean the leeks, discarding any coarse green tops and leaving the more tender pale green shoots; slice these thinly.

Heat the fat until melted, add the leeks and cook over a low heat until they are transparent. Add the stock, barley and bay leaves and season with salt and pepper. Bring to the boil, cover and simmer for about 20 minutes until the leeks are really tender and the barley is very soft. Add the chicken and milk and simmer for 3 minutes. Remove bay leaves.

Remove the tough stalks of the watercress (these can be used in the stock pot) and finely shred the leaves. Add the watercress leaves and cream to the soup and check the seasoning. Heat through without boiling and serve at once.

Kidney and Bacon Soup

Serves 4

2 lamb kidneys
2 rashers streaky bacon
1 large onion
1 teaspoon flour
2 pints (1 litre) beef stock
Salt, freshly-ground black pepper and a pinch allspice

3 tablespoons sherry
2 tablespoons double cream
1 tablespoon finely-chopped parsley

Remove the skin and core of the kidneys and cut the flesh
into very small dice. Remove the rind from the bacon and
chop the rashers. Peel and finely chop the onion.

Cook the bacon with the rinds but without extra fat, over
a low heat, until the fat has melted. Remove the rinds and
add the onion then continue to cook over a low heat until
the onion is soft. Raise the heat, add the kidney and cook
over a high heat until the kidney is browned on all sides.
Add the flour, mix well and cook until the flour has browned.
Blend in the stock, adding it gradually and stirring until the
soup comes to the boil and is thickened and smooth.
Season with salt and pepper and a pinch of allspice and
simmer for 30 minutes.

Add the sherry and the cream, heat through and mix in the
parsley just before serving.

Serendipity Soup

This is my soup and it hasn't been divulged to anyone before
now, so I feel a bit 'like that' about it. I made it up in the
summer of 1976 when, for the first time in my life, I actually
had more strawberries than I knew what to do with, and I
find it one of the most satisfactory starters I have ever
served. If you have a deep freeze, chill your soup bowls in it
before serving the soup – it must arrive at the table really
well chilled.

Serves 4

$\frac{1}{2}$ lb (225 g) ripe strawberries
$\frac{1}{2}$ pint (275 ml) water
1 chicken stock cube
$\frac{1}{2}$ teaspoon ground ginger
$\frac{1}{4}$ teaspoon ground turmeric

½ pint (275 ml) yoghurt
8 leaves mint
Salt and freshly-ground black pepper

Purée the fresh strawberries through a food mill or in a liquidiser. Combine the water and stock cube and heat through until the stock cube has completely melted. Mix well and leave to cool.

Take a little of the stock, add the ginger and turmeric and heat over a low flame, stirring continually until the spices are dissolved. Add the stock, spices and yoghurt to the strawberries and mix well. Add the mint, season with salt and pepper, chill well, pour into the iced soup bowls and serve well chilled.

2

Fresh from the Rivers, Streams and Coastline

Salmon and sea trout from the Tamar and Camel rivers; cockles and mussels from the sea shore and a wealth of marvellous fresh fish from the sea.

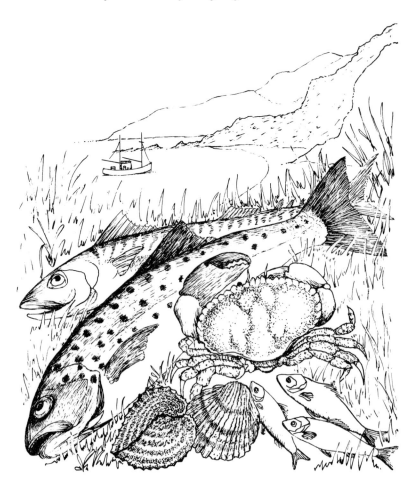

SAVOURY BUTTERS AND SAUCES TO
SERVE WITH FISH

SO MANY fish have such a bland and delicate flavour that, for some people, their taste is almost insignificant. Boiled, poached and grilled fish is greatly enhanced by a good sauce. With mackerel and other fish that tend to be on the rich and oily side a sharp sauce helps to counteract the oiliness and complement the flavour of the cooked ingredients.

Orange Paprika Butter

3 oz (75 g) butter
Grated rind of 1 orange
Juice of ½ orange
Salt
¼ teaspoon paprika

Beat the butter until creamy and beat in the orange rind, orange juice, a little salt and the paprika pepper. Shape into a sausage, wrap in tinfoil and chill in a refrigerator until hard. Cut into thin slices and serve with grilled mackerel, red mullet, John Dory etc.

Green Butter Sauce

2 large sprigs parsley
1 sprig fennel or dill
3 oz (75 g) butter
2 teaspoons lemon juice
Salt and freshly-ground black pepper

Plunge the parsley and fennel or dill into boiling water and cook for 5 minutes. Drain well, cool and chop very finely. Melt the butter in a small pan. Gradually beat in the lemon juice, add the parsley and fennel or dill, season with salt and freshly ground black pepper and serve at once.

   Serve with any fried, boiled or poached fish.

Gooseberry Sauce

    8 oz (225 g) green gooseberries
    2 tablespoons water
    2 oz (50 g) melted butter
    Pinch powdered ginger
    1 tablespoon caster sugar

Top and tail the gooseberries and cook with the water over a
low heat until tender. Put through a fine sieve or a food mill.
Combine them in a clean pan with the melted butter. Add
the ginger and sugar, bring to the boil and cook for 3
minutes. Serve with grilled or fried mackerel.

Mustard Sauce

    2 hard-boiled eggs
    1½ oz (40 g) butter
    2 tablespoons flour
    1½ teaspoons dry English mustard
    ¾ pint (425 ml) milk
    Salt and freshly-ground black pepper

Chop the hard-boiled eggs. Melt the butter in a saucepan.
Add the flour and mustard powder. Gradually add the milk,
stirring continually over a medium-high heat until the sauce
comes to the boil and is thick and smooth. Season with salt
and pepper and mix in the chopped hard-boiled eggs. Serve
with grilled or fried fish.

Parsley Sauce

The trouble with most parsley sauces is that they don't con-
tain enough parsley. The sauce should be bright green and
actually look like parsley and not like a white sauce speckled
with green leaves. When in doubt, use more finely-chopped
parsley than you think would be amply adequate. Serve with
chicken, fish, egg or vegetable dishes.

Serve the sauce with hard-boiled eggs, chicken (especially boiled chicken) or fish.

1 onion
4 cloves
2 bay leaves
¼ pint (150 ml) chicken stock (or stock cube and water)
¼ pint (150 ml) milk
1 large bunch parsley
1 oz (25 g) butter
1 tablespoon flour
1 teaspoon lemon juice
Salt and white pepper
1 tablespoon cream

Peel the onion and stick the cloves into it. Combine onion, bay leaves, stock and milk in a saucepan, bring to the boil and simmer gently for 15 minutes. Strain.

Remove the parsley stalks and very finely chop the leaves.

Heat the butter, add the flour and mix well. Gradually blend in the hot, strained liquid, stirring continually until the sauce is thick and smooth. Add the parsley and lemon juice, season with salt and pepper and add a little more milk if necessary. Mix in the cream just before serving.

Caper Sauce

Capers, like so many imported ingredients, used to be extremely expensive and beyond the means of most housewives. Nasturtium seeds pickled in vinegar with spices took their place and indeed it is hard to tell the difference.

Now that there is little mutton to be found, caper sauce is usually served with fish dishes of all kinds, but I have also found it delicious with boiled tongue and with roast or boiled chicken.

1 onion
4 cloves

2 bay leaves
$\frac{1}{4}$ pint (150 ml) chicken stock (or water and stock cube)
$\frac{1}{4}$ pint (150 ml) milk
1 oz (25 g) butter
1 oz (25 g) flour
2 tablespoons capers
Salt and freshly-ground black pepper
1 tablespoon cream

Peel the onion and stick the cloves in to it. Combine the onion, bay leaves, chicken stock and milk in a saucepan, bring to the boil and simmer for 15 minutes. Strain the liquid.

Melt the butter, add the flour and mix well. Gradually blend in the hot liquid, stirring continually until the sauce is thick and smooth. Add the capers (chop them if they are on the large side) season with salt and pepper and mix in the cream – do not boil after the capers have been added as the sauce might curdle.

Mussel Sauce

A cheaper sauce to make than the oyster variety and almost as delicious. I tried serving this with boiled chicken cut into thin slices and it was very good indeed.

1 dozen mussels
1 onion
4 cloves
$\frac{1}{4}$ pint (150 ml) chicken stock (or water and stock cube)
$\frac{1}{4}$ pint (150 ml) milk
2 bay leaves
1 oz (25 g) butter
1 oz (25 g) flour
Salt and freshly-ground black pepper
2 egg yolks
4 tablespoons cream

Scrub the mussels and remove their beards (see page 65). Place the mussels in a heavy pan, cover tightly and cook over a high heat without any liquid, shaking the pan every now and then. Heat for about 3 minutes until the mussels have opened wide. Strain off and reserve the liquid and remove the mussels from their shells.

Peel the onion and stick the cloves into it. Combine the stock, milk, onion and bay leaves in a saucepan and simmer for 15 minutes. Strain off the liquid.

Melt the butter in a saucepan, add the flour and mix well. Gradually blend in the hot liquid, stirring continually until the sauce comes to the boil and is thick and smooth. Add the mussel liquid and season with salt and pepper.

Beat the egg yolks with the cream until smooth. Add the egg and cream mixture to the sauce and heat through without boiling. Mix in the mussels and stir lightly, trying not to break up the shellfish.

Anchovy Sauce

Until the beginning of this century anchovies were imported in barrels, whole and salted and, on the whole, larger than those that are now used for tinned anchovy fillets. Now these can only be found in some Soho shops or on holidays abroad, but the tinned anchovy fillets make a good substitute. The taste of anchovies is one that could well do with a revival as it adds both flavour and a salt seasoning to a great many dishes, including those that have a basis of meat.

This sauce is delicious with any plainly cooked white fish.

6 anchovy fillets
$\frac{1}{4}$ pint (150 ml) water
$\frac{1}{4}$ pint (150 ml) white wine
Pared rind of 1 lemon
1 oz (25 g) butter
$1\frac{1}{2}$ teaspoons flour

    1 tablespoon white wine vinegar
    Freshly-ground black pepper
    1 teaspoon ground or finely-grated nutmeg
    2 tablespoons single cream

Drain the anchovies of oil and place them in a pan with the water, white wine and lemon rind. Bring to the boil and simmer for 10 minutes, pressing the anchovies with a wooden spoon to extract the flavour. Strain the liquid from the pan through a fine sieve.

    Melt the butter in a saucepan, add the flour and mix well. Gradually blend in the liquid from the pan, stirring continually until the mixture comes to the boil and is thick and smooth. Add the vinegar, season with pepper and nutmeg, mix well, blend in the cream and serve at once.

Note: An alternative sauce can be made by making a conventional white sauce, adding two very finely chopped anchovies and a finely-chopped hard-boiled egg and seasoning again with pepper and finely-grated nutmeg.

Oyster Sauce

Serve with plain boiled fish.

    8 small oysters
    Milk
    1 oz (25 g) butter
    2 tablespoons flour
    Lemon juice
    $\frac{1}{2}$ teaspoon anchovy essence
    Freshly-ground black pepper
    Pinch cayenne and ground nutmeg
    1 tablespoon finely-chopped parsley

Open the oysters, remove the beards, reserve and measure the liquor and cut each oyster into four. Add enough milk to the oyster liquor to make just over $\frac{1}{2}$ pint (275 ml).

Melt the butter in a saucepan. Add the flour and mix well. Gradually add the liquid, stirring continually over a medium high heat until the sauce is thick and smooth. Add lemon juice, season with the anchovy essence, pepper, a pinch of cayenne and a pinch of nutmeg and simmer for 10 minutes.

Add the oysters and parsley to the sauce, mix lightly and serve at once. If the sauce is too thick add a little more milk or a little cream.

Mackerel with Horseradish and Cider

Serves 4

4 medium-sized mackerel
2 teaspoons grated fresh horseradish root
1 teaspoon grated raw onion
4 oz (125 g) cream cheese
$\frac{1}{2}$ pint (275 ml) medium dry cider
Salt and freshly-ground black pepper
4 bay leaves

Gut and clean the fish but leave the heads and tails on. Work the horseradish and onion into the cream cheese with two tablespoons of cider until the mixture is smooth. Spread the cheese mixture inside each fish and arrange them head to tail in a lightly-greased fireproof dish. Season with a little salt and pepper, place a bay leaf on each fish and pour over the remaining cider.

Cover the dish tightly with tinfoil and bake in a moderate oven (350° F, Reg 4) for 40 minutes.

Smoked Mackerel and Cream Cheese Pâté with Walnuts

Serves 4

1 smoked mackerel (medium size)
4 oz (125 g) butter
4 oz (125 g) cream cheese
Juice ½ lemon
½ teaspoon grated raw onion
Salt and freshly-ground black pepper
Pinch cayenne
2 oz (50 g) walnuts

Remove the skin of the mackerel and fillet the fish. Flake the flesh of the mackerel. Heat the butter until just foaming, add the flaked mackerel and either pound to a smooth purée or put through a food mill or liquidiser. Cool the mixture and beat in the cream cheese, lemon juice and grated raw onion. Season with salt, pepper and a pinch of cayenne.

Finely chop the walnuts, mix them into the pâté and divide the mixture between small ramekin dishes. Serve the pâté with hot toast.

Marinated Mackerel

Serves 4

4 mackerel
10 peppercorns
1 large onion
Pinch mace
4 cloves
4 bay leaves
Pinch allspice
Sprig thyme
2 sage leaves
Salt and white wine vinegar

Cut, clean and remove the heads and tails of the mackerel. Carefully remove the backbones and arrange the fish in a lightly-greased baking dish. Cover the fish with the peppercorns, the onion peeled and cut into rings, the herbs and spices. Season generously with salt and just cover with vinegar. Cover with greaseproof paper or foil and bake in a moderate oven (350° F, Reg 4) for 40 minutes.

Carefully lift out the fish, removing any of the flavouring ingredients, place in a clean dish and strain over the vinegar mixture. Cool and then chill and serve neatly rolled up.

Salmagundy

When people took religion seriously, Salmagundy was a dish served on Ash Wednesday or other days in Lent. It wasn't just the prerogative of the Roman Catholics either, as Protestants and other religious sects treated Lent with respect and this was a popular Lenten dish that, dare I say it, has many similarities to Jewish dishes.

Anyway, far be it from me to preach religion and whatever your faith, Salmagundy makes a delicious salad meal at any time. It used to be made with salted, soaked herring, but now these are no longer readily available (another symptom of our twentieth-century civilization!) so I have used West Country mackerel in this dish, and it is very good indeed.

Serve the Salmagundy as a first course, or as a main course in the summer for lunch or supper.

One of the secrets of this dish has always been the way it is presented with everything separately divided into compartments. Originally they were served on separate plates but I prefer them all together on a large platter.

Serves 4

2 smoked mackerel
1 cucumber
2 crisp eating apples
2 shallots or, better still, 4 spring onions

2 dill-pickled cucumbers
2 hard-boiled eggs
1 bunch watercress
3 tablespoons pickled red cabbage
Nasturtium flowers if available
6 tablespoons olive oil
2 tablespoons white wine vinegar
1 teaspoon French Dijon mustard
Salt and freshly-ground black pepper

Skin the smoked mackerel and remove the bones. Flake the flesh with a fork and arrange the mackerel in the centre of a serving dish. Peel and thinly slice the cucumber. Peel and core the apple and cut the flesh into small dice. Peel and finely chop the shallots or spring onions. Chop the dill-pickled cucumbers and eggs and remove the stalks from the watercress. Arrange all the ingredients around the smoked mackerel.

Combine the oil, vinegar, mustard and seasoning in a screw-topped jar and shake to mix well. Pour the dressing over all the ingredients and chill in a refrigerator before serving.

Note: This dish is one where you can really let your imagination rip. Include cold boiled new potatoes, cut into small dice, or baby beetroot, young French beans or any other delicious things you have in the garden. Basically, as long as a marinated mackerel, herring or smoked flaked fish is in the centre it can consist of any salad combination.

JOHN DORY

This is a fish special to the West Country and, to my mind, equal to turbot in texture and flavour. It's a fleshy, fat fish and easily recognised by the dark 'finger and thumb' spot on its flanks. Legend has it that St Peter, fishing, caught a John Dory and the fish groaned so loudly at having been captured that St Peter picked it up between his finger and thumb and threw it back into the water, freeing the fish but leaving it branded for ever with the mark of the Apostle. Like dabs, the John Dory is so special it should not be served in any other than the most simple of ways. Like turbot, it is delicious cold with a mayonnaise sauce.

Serves 6

1 John Dory weighing about 5 lb (2·3 kg)
Water and white wine
Bouquet garni of a sprig of parsley, thyme and sage
    with 2 or 3 bay leaves
1 onion
½ lemon
Salt and 8 peppercorns
1 tablespoon olive oil

Place the John Dory in a fish kettle and just cover with equal quantities of water and dry white wine (the wine need not be of exceptional quality; substitute dry cider if times are hard). Add bouquet garni, olive oil, onion, peeled and sliced, and the lemon, cut into thick slices. Season with a little salt and throw in the peppercorns. Bring to the boil slowly and simmer, with the water just moving, for about 20 minutes or until the flesh of the fish is just coming away from the bone.

Lift out the fish, garnish it with fresh lemon slices and serve with boiled potatoes, a green vegetable and a tartare or Hollandaise sauce.

Cold John Dory with Mayonnaise

Serves 8

Follow the instructions for the John Dory recipe, but remove the fish from the heat as soon as the liquid comes to the boil. Leave to cool in the liquid in which it was cooked.

Lift out the fish, remove the skin and then carefully remove the flesh from the bones. Arrange the flesh on a serving dish and mask with ½ pint (275 ml) home-made mayonnaise. Garnish with wedges of lemon and a few peeled prawns and serve with a potato and green salad.

Lemon Sole in Creamy Sauce

Serves 4

4 lemon soles, filleted, with the bones
½ pint (275 ml) cider
½ pint (275 ml) water
2 onions
Bouquet garni
Blade mace
Pinch cayenne
Salt and freshly-ground black pepper
Juice of ½ lemon
2 oz (50 g) butter
1½ tablespoons flour
4 tablespoons cream
1 tablespoon finely-chopped parsley

Remove the black skin from the fillets by laying the fillet flat and sliding a sharp knife between the flesh and skin. Put the skin, head and bones into a saucepan. Cover with the cider and water, add one onion, peeled and sliced, the bouquet garni, mace and a pinch of cayenne, season with salt and pepper, bring to the boil and simmer for 30 minutes. Strain off the stock and measure ¾ pint (425 ml).

Arrange the fillets in a well-greased baking dish. Sprinkle with lemon juice and a little salt and pepper and dot with ½ oz (15 g) of butter. Cover with greaseproof paper and bake in a moderate oven (350° F, Reg 4) for 10 minutes.

Peel and finely chop the remaining onion. Melt the remaining 1½ oz (40 g) of butter in a saucepan. Add the onion and cook over a low heat until the onion is soft and transparent. Add the flour and mix well and gradually blend in the fish stock, stirring continually over a high heat until the sauce comes to the boil and is thick and smooth. Simmer for 3 minutes, then remove from the heat and blend in the cream and parsley. Season with salt and pepper if necessary, pour the sauce over the fish and serve at once.

Dabs with Parsley

Autumn is the best time to find dabs, small flat fish with flesh that is just as good as a Dover sole and of a size that is usually far more manageable. Fresh dabs are so good that I think it is a pity to dress them up in any way; they respond beautifully to being fried or grilled and served with wedges of lemon. Crisp, fried, parsley sprigs also go well with simple fried fish like this.

Serves 4

4 dabs (dabs are bought cleaned from the fishmongers
    with the intestine pulled through a slit below the gills)
1 egg, beaten
Browned breadcrumbs
2 oz (50 g) butter
2 tablespoons olive oil
8 sprigs parsley
Salt and freshly-ground black pepper
Quarters of lemon

Dip the dabs, complete with heads and tails, in beaten egg and then in a coating of breadcrumbs.

Heat the butter with the oil, in a large frying pan, until bubbling. Add the dabs and cook over a high heat for 4 minutes, turn over and cook for a further 4 minutes on the other side. Remove the fish, drain on kitchen paper and keep warm.

Remove most of the stems from the parsley sprigs, leaving the crowns whole. Fry the sprigs in the hot fat in the frying pan until they are crisp. Drain on kitchen paper.

Pour the juices from the pan through a sieve into a sauce boat, season with salt and pepper and serve with the dabs, garnished with the fried sprigs of parsley and lemon wedges.

Stuffed Gurnards in Jackets

Gurnards are the sort of fish that one would not like to come face to face with on a dark night. Their dog-shaped snouts and bewhiskered jaws are positively frightening to look at but, if you can ignore their lack of beauty and cope with their many bones, the flesh is not unlike that of a red mullet and just as delicious.

Gurnards are often plentiful in the coastal villages and markets of the West Country, especially Cornwall, and are very good cooked the same way as red mullet, stuffed with herbs and wrapped in greaseproof paper. Bake the gurnards in a moderate oven (350° F, Reg 4) for 20 minutes for a small fish or 40 minutes for a large fish weighing 2–3 lb (1–1½ kg).

Traditionally the fish are served with a well-flavoured parsley sauce (see page 32).

Grilled Salmon with Butter and Parsley

This is one of those beautiful simple dishes that one remembers and dreams about when away from the golden sands and windswept coasts of the West.

Serves 4

4 oz (125 g) butter
Salt and freshly-ground black pepper
4 salmon cutlets cut from the middle of the salmon and
    about ½ in (1 cm) thick
3 oz (75 g) small button mushrooms
2 tablespoons thick cream
½ teaspoon lemon juice
2 tablespoons finely-chopped parsley

Line a grill pan with foil and rub the foil with a little of the butter. Lightly season the salmon steaks and lay them in the pan. Melt half the remaining butter, pour it over the steaks and grill them under a medium high heat for 5 minutes.

Thinly slice the mushrooms. Turn the steaks over, stuff the stomach end of the steaks with sliced mushrooms, baste with the juice in the pan and return to the grill for a further 3 minutes until the salmon flesh is just coming away from the bone. Remove the steaks, using a wide spatula so that the mushrooms remain in place, on to a heated serving dish, pour the thick cream over the mushrooms and keep warm while making the sauce.

Pour the juices from the pan into a saucepan. Add the remaining butter and heat until it has melted. Stir in the lemon juice and parsley, season if necessary with a little more salt and pepper and heat through.

Pour the sauce over the main part of the steaks (the cream should have warmed by then but not become runny enough to spread so that the mushrooms have their cream sauce and the fish is generously smothered in the savoury butter).

Serve the fish with new or baked potatoes and a light-tasting green vegetable (nothing too strongly flavoured) or a salad.

Grilled Marinated Salmon Steaks

Salmon tends to dry out when it is cut into steaks. This method of marinating the steaks prevents this happening and produces dishes that do justice to this delicious fish. The vinegar can be reboiled, strained and used again.

Serves 6

1 shallot or small onion
1 pint (575 ml) white wine vinegar
1 blade mace
3 cloves

8 peppercorns
6 salmon steaks
1 tablespoon olive oil

Clean but do not peel the shallot and cut it into quarters. Combine the vinegar, shallot, mace, cloves and peppercorns in a saucepan, bring to the boil and remove at once from the heat. Leave to cool and then strain through a fine sieve. Place the steaks in a shallow dish, pour over the cold vinegar, add the olive oil and leave to stand for 30 minutes. Drain off the liquid and cook the steaks under a medium hot grill for about 4 minutes on each side until the flesh is just flaking off the bones.

Serve with mayonnaise or Hollandaise sauce.

Salmon Fishcakes

If you are fortunate enough to have access to a whole salmon you will almost certainly end up with some left over from a whole fish that has been served cold. Use it to make a delicious kedgeree or these very superior fishcakes that are a very special breakfast dish, or a rewarding lunch or supper dish when accompanied by a tomato sauce and a mixed salad.

Serves 4

1 small onion
$\frac{1}{2}$ oz (15 g) butter
8 oz (225 g) cooked salmon
8 oz (225 g) cold mashed potatoes
1 tablespoon finely-chopped parsley
Salt and freshly-ground black pepper
1 egg, beaten
Dried breadcrumbs
Lard or cooking oil

Peel and finely chop the onion. Cook onion in the butter over a low heat until the onion is soft and transparent. Flake the fish. Add the fish to the mashed potatoes with the parsley, onion and juices from the pan. Season with salt and pepper and mix lightly until the mixture is firm. Form into flat cakes about 3 in (8 cm) wide and $\frac{1}{4}$ in ($\frac{1}{2}$ cm) thick and dip each cake into the beaten egg and then into dried bread-crumbs. Fry in hot lard or a little cooking oil until crisp and golden brown on both sides. Drain on kitchen paper.

Baked Red Mullet

Known as the woodcock of the sea, red mullet are plentiful around the coast of Cornwall. For some reason these delicious fish are not as popular in England as they are in France, although I have sometimes had them well cooked in some of the few good Cornish restaurants. Much of their flavour lies in cooking them, like woodcock, with the entrails still in the body. Don't be put off by this idea – the fish are clean eaters and the guts merely provide a delicious flavour to the fish.

This is an old recipe and must, I imagine, have originated in France. Probably it came to Cornwall with the Breton sailors who have always plied between the two countries.

Serves 4

$4\frac{1}{2}$–$4\frac{3}{4}$ lb (2 kg) red mullet
4 ripe tomatoes
2 oz (50 g) fat cooked ham
2 shallots
2 tablespoons finely-chopped parsley
2 oz (50 g) coarsely grated Cheddar cheese
2 anchovy fillets
Salt and freshly-ground black pepper
$\frac{1}{2}$ pint (275 ml) white wine or dry cider
$\frac{1}{2}$ oz (15 g) butter
1 tablespoon flour
2 teaspoons capers
Pinch of cayenne pepper

Wash and dry but do not gut the mullet. Dip the tomatoes into boiling water for 2 minutes, slide off the skin, halve and remove any tough core and roughly chop the flesh. Very finely chop the ham. Peel and chop the shallots.

Arrange the mullet in a greased baking dish. Spread over the parsley, tomato, ham, cheese and chopped anchovy fillets. Season with pepper, pour over the wine or cider, cover with foil and bake in a moderately hot oven (375° F, Reg 5) for 20 minutes until the flesh is just coming away from the bone. Scrape off the ingredients over the mullet, remove the fish carefully to a heated serving dish and keep warm. Purée the ingredients from the baking dish with the wine through a sieve or a food mill.

Melt the butter in a saucepan. Add the flour and mix well. Add the puréed liquid, stirring continually over a medium heat until the sauce comes to the boil and is thick and smooth. Mix in the capers, add a little cayenne and taste for seasoning. Pour the sauce over the fish and serve at once.

Piquant Whitings

I have never really liked the fashion of serving whitings with the heads biting at their tails. As a child I used to feel so sorry for the fish I could not bear to look at them, let alone eat the poor things. But these are good fish, and this less traditional way of cooking them is well worth trying.

Serves 4

4 medium whitings
1 shallot or small onion
Salt and freshly-ground black pepper
2 bay leaves
Juice of 1 lemon
¼ pint (150 ml) white wine
¼ pint (150 ml) water
2 oz (50 g) butter
2 teaspoons finely-chopped parsley

Remove the heads and tails of the whitings, lay them flat and cut a couple of nicks through the backbones to prevent them curling up while cooking. Peel and finely chop the shallot or onion. Butter a shallow baking dish, lay the whitings on the dish, side by side, and sprinkle over the shallot or onion. Season with salt and pepper, add the bay leaves, pour over the lemon juice, wine and water and dot the fish with butter.

Bake the fish, uncovered, in a moderate oven (350° F, Reg 4) for 20 minutes, basting frequently, until the fish are beginning to flake from the backbone and most of the juices in the baking dish have been absorbed. Sprinkle with the chopped parsley and serve at once.

West Country Hors d'Oeuvres

This is my interpretation of a dish sometimes served during the summer at the Horn of Plenty restaurant in Gunnislake, Devon.

Serves 4

1 crisp eating apple
1 cooked potato
2 chipples or spring onions
½ pint (275 ml) home-made mayonnaise
Salt and freshly-ground black pepper
4 hard-boiled eggs
8 thin slices black pudding
Dripping
4 small marinated pilchards (see page 52) or 4 marinated mackerel fillets (see page 38)

Peel, core and cut the apple into small dice. Cut the potato into small dice. Clean and chop the chipples or spring onions. Combine the apple, potato and onion with half the mayonnaise and mix lightly; season with salt and pepper.

Halve the hard-boiled eggs. Cook the black pudding

slices in hot dripping for about 3 minutes on each side until crisp. Drain on kitchen paper.

Arrange the marinated pilchards or marinated mackerel fillets on four plates. Place a mound of apple and potato salad, a hard-boiled egg, cut sides down, and two black pudding slices on each plate and mask the hard-boiled eggs with the remaining mayonnaise.

Serve chilled with brown bread and butter.

Breakfast Fishcakes

This is taken from a recipe of the turn of the century. It is unpretentious and is another 'breakfast' recipe that, in these days, adapts well to a light supper.

Please, I beg of you, use fresh breadcrumbs, not that goldfish food that comes in packets.

Serves 6

1 lb (450 g) cooked white fish
2 lb (900 g) cold mashed potato
Juice $\frac{1}{2}$ lemon
Grated rind of $\frac{1}{4}$ lemon
1 tablespoon finely-chopped parsley
2 teaspoons anchovy essence
Pinch of cayenne pepper
Salt
1 egg, beaten
Finely-grated fresh white breadcrumbs
Bacon fat or dripping

Flake the fish with a fork and mix it with the potato, lemon juice, lemon rind, parsley and anchovy essence. Season with a little cayenne and some salt and mix really well. Form into flat cakes, $\frac{1}{4}$ in ($\frac{1}{2}$ cm) thick and 2 in (5 cm) across. Dip the cakes in beaten egg and press into the breadcrumbs so that crumbs are evenly distributed on both sides. Chill for 30 minutes.

Cook the cakes in bacon fat or clean dripping until crisp and golden brown on both sides.

Note: I like these served with a home-made tomato sauce and crisply-fried sprigs of parsley (see page 115).

Kedgeree Revival

Kedgeree used to be a breakfast dish in the good old days when our grandfathers seem to have eaten four square meals a day and the dreaded scales didn't feature much in day-to-day living. In 1978 kedgeree has taken a new place as a more savoury dish that can be served for lunch or supper.

Serves 4

1 lb (450 g) smoked haddock or cod fillets
½ pint (275 ml) milk
8 oz (225 g) long grained rice
2 hard-boiled eggs
1 large onion
2 oz (50 g) butter
1 egg
¼ pint (150 ml) single cream
Freshly-ground black pepper
Finely-chopped parsley

Lightly butter a large frying pan. Lay the smoked fish fillets skin side down in the pan and pour over the milk. Add enough water to cover the fish, bring gently to the boil, cover and simmer for 10–15 minutes until the fish is tender and will flake easily. Drain off the milk, remove any skin and bones and flake the fish with a fork.

Cook the rice in boiling salted water until just tender. Drain and rinse through with cold water to remove excess starch. Drain well, spread on a plate and put into a slow oven for about 15 minutes to allow the rice to dry.

Roughly chop the hard-boiled eggs. Peel and chop the

onion. Melt the butter in a large frying pan over a low heat. Add the onion and cook slowly until the onion is soft and transparent. Add the rice and haddock and mix lightly until all the ingredients are hot through. Gently mix in the chopped hard-boiled eggs.

Combine the raw egg with the cream and mix until smooth. Add to the fish and rice mixture, season generously with pepper and mix lightly until the kedgeree is hot and creamy. Serve at once sprinkled with plenty of finely-chopped parsley.

Marinated Pilchards

In the days of wood-powered baking ovens this dish would have been put into the oven after the baking was done and left to stew slowly all night. The fish should be cooked until the bones have all softened completely and the fish need not be filleted before eating.

Serves 4

4 small pilchards
Salt and freshly-ground black pepper
4 bay leaves
Malt vinegar
1 onion

Remove the heads and tails from the pilchards and gut the fish. Season inside and out with salt and pepper and place a bay leaf inside each fish.

Place the fish, side by side, in an earthenware baking dish and pour over enough vinegar to cover. Peel and thinly slice the onion and place the slices on top of the fish. Cover tightly with foil and cook in a slow oven (300° F, Reg 2) for 3 hours. Leave to cool in the vinegar liquid and when quite cold, remove and serve well chilled with horseradish sauce.

Baked Spiced Pilchards

This versatile dish can also be made with herrings or mackerel.

Serves 4

8 pilchards
$\frac{1}{4}$ teaspoon ground cloves
$\frac{1}{2}$ teaspoon allspice
$\frac{1}{8}$ teaspoon salt
$\frac{1}{8}$ teaspoon freshly-ground black pepper
1 onion
8 small bay leaves
$\frac{1}{4}$ pint (150 ml) white wine vinegar
$\frac{1}{2}$ pint (275 ml) medium dry cider

Clean and fillet the fish or ask your fishmonger to do this for you. Lay the fillets out flat.

Combine the ground cloves, allspice, salt and pepper and mix well. Rub the spices over the cut side of each fillet and roll up tightly. Pack the rolled fillets closely in a lightly-greased fireproof dish.

Peel and thinly slice the onion and divide into rings. Arrange the onion rings and bay leaves over the rolled fillets and pour over the vinegar and cider. Cover the dish tightly with foil and bake in a moderate oven (350° F, Reg 4) for 45 minutes.

Serve hot with potatoes and a green vegetable or cold with salad.

Soused Sprats

A good economical first course for those warmer October evenings when sprats are cheap and plentiful.

Serves 4

2 pints (1 litre) dry cider
1 onion
6 peppercorns
Pinch salt
1 bay leaf
Small sprig thyme
1½ lb (675 g) sprats

Boil the cider over a high heat until it is reduced by half. Leave to cool. Peel the onion, cut it into thin slices and divide into rings.

Add the onion, peppercorns, salt, bay leaf and thyme to the cider.

Wash and dry the sprats but do not remove the heads or tails or gut them. Arrange in a lightly-greased shallow baking dish and pour over the marinade. Cover with foil and bake in a moderate oven (350° F, Reg 4) for 40 minutes.

Leave to cool in the marinating liquid and serve chilled with buttered brown bread, wedges of lemon and a horse-radish sauce.

Dry Fried Sprats

One of the things that puts people off sprats is their peculiarly fatty nature. In this recipe the sprats are fried dry with salt. The salt draws out the fat, providing their own natural cooking liquor.

Serves 4

1½ lb (675 g) sprats
Flour

3 teaspoons salt
Lemon wedges

Wash the sprats well and dry on kitchen paper. Put them
in a paper bag with plenty of flour and shake the bag well
until the sprats are coated in flour on all sides.

Put the salt in a heavy frying pan over a low heat. Shake
the pan to spread the salt evenly and leave for 2 minutes
to heat. Arrange the fish over the salt and cook over a high
heat, for 3 minutes on each side until the sprats are cooked
through and brown on each side.

Serve with buttered slices of brown bread and wedges of
lemon.

Squid Salad

One of my favourite ways of serving squid is to cook it
lightly and serve as a fish salad. Sometimes I add prawns
and occasionally hens (shellfish similar to the small clams
found on the coast of Portugal) but usually the squid make
up the basis of the salad.

Serves 4

1 lb (450 g) small squid
6 tablespoons olive oil
1 tablespoon white wine vinegar
1 teaspoon Dijon mustard
1 small clove garlic
1 tablespoon finely-chopped parsley
Salt and freshly-ground black pepper
2 ripe firm tomatoes
1 green pepper
1 onion
1 tablespoon tomato ketchup

Pull off the heads of the squid and cut off the tentacles just
in front of the eyes. Using fingernails, scrape off the pulpy
skin from the tentacles. Using a sharp knife, slit the body

of the squid from top to bottom. Scrape out and discard the intestine and pull off the purplish skin from the body and fins. Wash the squid in cold, slightly salted water and pat dry on kitchen paper. Cut the body into very thin strips, or into squares about 2 in (5 cm) across, and then score the flesh, three-quarters of the way through, in a criss-cross pattern.

Heat 2 tablespoons of olive oil in a heavy frying pan until smoking. Add the squid and cook over a high heat until the flesh curls up and becomes opaque. Remove at once with a slotted spoon, reserve the juices in the pan and leave squid and juices to cool.

Combine 4 tablespoons olive oil with the vinegar, mustard, crushed garlic, parsley, salt and pepper in a screw-topped jar and shake to mix well. Blend in the juices from the pan and mix well.

Cover the tomatoes with boiling water, leave for 2 minutes and then slide off the skins. Remove the core and seeds and chop the flesh. Remove the core and seeds of the green pepper and finely chop the flesh. Peel and finely chop the onion.

Combine the squid with the vegetables, tomato ketchup and dressing, toss lightly and chill before serving.

Note: For a more substantial main course salad, add 4 oz (125 g) peeled prawns and serve on a bed of crisp lettuce leaves.

EELS

These days the most usual place to find conger eel is on a fishmonger's slab disguised as cod steaks. The average British housewife I'm told, doesn't 'fancy' conger, but will eat it happily under the name of cod. Since it tastes similar and has rather the same texture I suppose there is no reason why she shouldn't remain in ignorance.

Eel Pie

Eel pie used to be very popular along the coasts and in small inland inns. The eels were thought to be very nutritious and the pie was said to be as good cold as it was hot. Conger eel can be used, but will need boning before cooking and cutting into small dice.

Serves 4–6

1½ lb (675 g) eels
2 shallots
3 sprigs parsley
½ pint (275 ml) white wine
Salt, freshly-ground black pepper and nutmeg
Milk
3 hard-boiled eggs
½ oz (15 g) butter
2 tablespoons flour
Juice of 1 lemon
4 tablespoons finely-chopped parsley
½ lb (225 g) puff pastry

Ask your fishmonger to clean and skin the eels. Cut them into 1 in (2½ cm) pieces and remove the bones if the eels are over 1 in (2½ cm) in diameter. Peel and finely chop the shallots. Combine the sprigs of parsley in a saucepan with the white wine, place the pieces of eel on top and pour over some water, if necessary, to cover. Season with salt, pepper and nutmeg. Bring to the boil and simmer, uncovered, for about 30 minutes or until the eels are tender and coming off the bone (this depends on their size).

Take out the pieces of eel, keep them warm and strain the stock. Add enough milk to the stock to make ¾ pint (425 ml) of liquid. Chop the hard-boiled eggs. Melt the butter in a saucepan, add the flour and mix well. Gradually blend in the strained stock, stirring continually until the sauce is thick and smooth. Bring to the boil and simmer for 3 minutes. Add the lemon juice, parsley and chopped eggs and mix lightly. Add the eel, turn into a pie dish and top with the puff pastry rolled out to just under $\frac{1}{4}$ in (6 mm) thickness. Brush with beaten egg and bake in a hot oven (425° F, Reg 7) for 10 minutes then lower the heat to moderate (350° F, Reg 4) and continue to bake for a further 30 minutes.

Wine-stewed Conger Eel

I have a feeling that eel is again going to become the popular dish that it once was, despite its unattractive appearance. The flesh and flavour are not unlike that of cod, but the price should be very much lower.

Serves 5–6

2 lb (900 g) conger eel (middle cut)
3 oz (75 g) butter
2 fillets anchovy
1 tablespoon grated raw horseradish
1 medium onion
2 tablespoons flour
$\frac{1}{2}$ pint (275 ml) stock (chicken or fish)
$\frac{1}{4}$ pint (150 ml) red wine
Freshly-ground black pepper
3 tablespoons finely-chopped parsley

Remove the skin from the cleaned eel (use a sharp pointed knife and slide the point inside the skin) and cut the eel off the backbone. Cut the filleted eel into 1 in (2$\frac{1}{2}$ cm) cubes.

Melt 2 oz (50 g) butter in a heavy pan. Add the eel and cook over a moderately high heat, shaking the pan to prevent burning, for about 20 minutes until the eel is tender.

Pound the anchovy to a paste with the grated horseradish. Peel and thinly slice the onion. Melt remaining butter in a saucepan, add the onion and cook over a low heat until soft and transparent. Add the flour, anchovy and horseradish and mix well. Gradually add the stock and wine, stirring continually over a medium high heat until the sauce is thick and smooth. Bring to the boil, season with pepper and simmer for 3 minutes. Add the eel and parsley and heat through.

Elvers

Elvers were known as the whitebait of the sea and thought to be so nutritious that a plateful was considered to be an ample meal for a working man. These small, immature eels, like silver threads, should be cooked in the same way as whitebait. They are to be found in the Severn area and were once hawked round the streets in large barrels.

Serves 4

1 lb (450 g) elvers
Flour
Salt
Freshly-ground black pepper and a pinch of cayenne
Deep fat or vegetable oil for frying

Wash the elvers in plenty of salted water, drain and pat dry on kitchen paper. Dip the elvers in flour seasoned with salt, pepper and a pinch of cayenne. Fry the elvers in very hot fat or vegetable oil until they are golden and crisp throughout (about 4 minutes). Do not fry too many of the elvers at one time and drain them well on kitchen paper.

Eat as soon as possible with wedges of lemon, buttered slices of brown bread and tartare sauce.

COCKLES

Clean cockles or clams by covering them with cold water which you change every 6 hours for 24–36 hours (as with oysters you can fatten the shellfish by adding a handful of porridge oats to the water). Drain the shellfish well and open them by putting them into a very large pan, without extra water, over a high heat and shaking the pan until the shellfish open.

I find the cockles good to serve just as they are, in a salad with a dressing of oil, vinegar, seasoning and finely-chopped parsley and chives. They can also be used in that delicious Italian *spaghetti alle vongole* (spaghetti dressed with butter in which some cockles have been heated with seasoning), in a fish cocktail, or in a cream sauce like scallops – serve in a scallop shell.

New Potato and Cockle Salad

Serves 4

1 lb (450 g) peeled and cooked new potatoes
2 chipples or spring onions
$\frac{1}{4}$ pint (150 ml) home-made mayonnaise
2 tablespoons tomato ketchup
$\frac{1}{2}$ teaspoon Worcestershire sauce
1 teaspoon lemon juice
2 tablespoons double cream
Salt and freshly-ground black pepper
$\frac{1}{4}$ pint (150 ml) cockles
1 lettuce heart
Cayenne pepper

Cut the potatoes into small dice. Very finely chop the chipples. Combine the mayonnaise, tomato ketchup, Worcestershire sauce, lemon juice and cream, season with salt and pepper and mix well. Add the potatoes, cockles and chipples to the mayonnaise mixture and mix lightly.

Chop the lettuce heart and arrange it in the bottom of four glasses or small bowls, spoon over the salad and sprinkle with a little cayenne.

Serve chilled with buttered brown bread.

Penzance Cockle Pie

Serves 4

3 fillets anchovies
3 oz (75 g) butter
1½ tablespoons flour
¾ pint (425 ml) milk
Freshly-ground black pepper and a pinch of nutmeg
1½ lb (675 g) shelled cockles
2 tablespoons finely-chopped parsley
3 oz (75 g) white breadcrumbs browned in the oven
   (see below)
¾ lb (350 g) cold mashed potatoes

Drain and mash the anchovies with a fork. Melt 1 oz (25 g) of butter. Add the flour and mix well. Gradually add the milk, stirring continually over a medium high heat until the mixture comes to the boil and is thick and smooth. Season with pepper and a little nutmeg, add the mashed anchovies, mix well and simmer for 5 minutes. Add the cockles and parsley and mix well.

Spread half the breadcrumbs over the bottom of a lightly-greased baking dish. Cover with half the cockle sauce mixture, top with remaining breadcrumbs and finally spread over the remaining cockle mixture. Cover the dish with a layer of mashed potatoes, top with remaining butter cut into small pieces and bake in a moderate oven (375° F, Reg 5) for 20 minutes or until the top is lightly browned and crisp.

Browning White Breadcrumbs

Cut the crusts from slices of stale bread. Bake them in a low oven (do this when there is something already cooking at a slow heat and the bread can be put into the bottom of the oven) for about 2 hours or until the bread is crisp throughout and a golden brown in colour. If you own an Aga this can be done in the bottom left-hand oven.

Cool the bread and then crush with a rolling pin into fine breadcrumbs. Breadcrumbs can also be made in an electric liquidiser but take care not to process so much that the crumbs become too fine.

SCALLOPS

I love these pink and white shellfish so much that I find it difficult to know which is the best way to cook them – almost completely plain, just gently cooked in butter with a sprinkling of parsley, lemon juice, salt and freshly-ground black pepper; in the rich garlic and tomato sauce of Provence, or encased in a rich cheese sauce and served in a ring of mashed potatoes with the dish being lightly browned under a hot grill just before serving.

Scallops in Saffron Sauce

Serves 4–6

12 scallops
4 oz (125 g) cooked well-drained leaf spinach
1 onion
1 oz (25 g) butter
½ pint (275 ml) chicken stock (or water and stock cube)
½ teaspoon powdered saffron
1 bay leaf
Salt and freshly-ground black pepper
1 heaped tablespoon plain flour
½ pint (275 ml) milk
2 egg yolks
2 tablespoons finely-chopped parsley
2 oz (50 g) fine white breadcrumbs
A little melted butter

Separate the pink coral from the white disc of the scallops, remove the black vein running around the side, wash them under cold running water and leave to drain. Leave the pink coral whole and slice the white part into $\frac{1}{4}$ in ($\frac{1}{2}$ cm) thick slices. Finely chop the spinach. Peel and finely chop the onion and cook it over a low heat in a little of the butter until soft and transparent.

Add the chicken stock, saffron and bay leaf, season with salt and pepper, bring to the boil and simmer gently for 20 minutes. Remove the bay leaf.

Melt the remaining butter in a heavy pan. Add the flour and mix well. Gradually blend in the milk, stirring continuously over a medium heat until the sauce is thick and smooth. Add all but 2 tablespoons of the chicken stock, stir well and simmer gently for 5 minutes.

Beat the egg yolks until smooth, blend in the reserved chicken stock and then add the mixture to the sauce, beating well. Cook for 3 minutes without boiling and remove from the heat.

Mix the scallops, parsley and spinach into the sauce and pour into a fireproof serving dish. Spread the breadcrumbs over the surface, dribble over some melted butter and put into a moderate oven (400° F, Reg 6) for 10 minutes until the top is golden brown.

Serve with rice and salad as a main course. As a first course serve in scallop shells or ramekin dishes.

Scallops with Bacon

This is one of the best fish/meat combinations. The bacon and scallops complement each other perfectly both in flavour and texture and can be combined in many different ways.

Serves 4

12 medium-sized scallops
4 rashers thinly sliced streaky bacon
2 shallots or 1 small onion
$1\frac{1}{2}$ oz (40 g) butter

1 tablespoon lemon juice
Salt and freshly-ground black pepper
1 tablespoon finely-chopped parsley
3 tablespoons medium dry sherry

Slide scallops on the shell off by scraping a sharp knife along the bottom of the scallops. Remove the tough muscle at the side and detach and discard the thin black line running around the side of each scallop. Wash the scallops in cold water and pat them dry with kitchen paper.

Cut each scallop into three pieces, keeping the red coral intact. Remove the rinds from the rashers and chop the bacon into small pieces. Peel and finely chop the shallots or onion.

Melt half the butter in a heavy frying pan. Add the bacon and onion and cook over a low heat, stirring now and then, for about 5 minutes or until the onion is golden brown. Add the remaining butter and as soon as it is melted add the scallops and lemon juice. Season with salt and pepper and cook over a medium heat for 5 minutes. Stir in the parsley and transfer the ingredients to a serving dish. Add the sherry to any juices left in the pan, stir until it boils and then pour it over the scallops and serve at once.

MUSSELS

Mussels are still to be had for the picking along the West Country coastline. You want to be careful where you pick them though. Those near sewer outlets are often the largest but in no way the best. Mussels, like all shellfish, while thriving on the more sordid side of life, also become contaminated by the poisons they pick up.

Collect your mussels from a clean shore line, pulling them off the rocks when the tide is out. Put them in a bucket of fresh water with a handful of salt and a handful of oatmeal and leave them to stand for 24 hours before cleaning and cooking – this will help to clean the shellfish of sand and other impurities.

Discard any mussels that are open and do not immediately close very tightly when tapped. Such shellfish are dangerous and could well lead to shellfish poisoning if they are eaten.

Mussels Maidenwell

Serves 4

2 quarts (2 litres) mussels
2 shallots
$\frac{1}{2}$ pint (275 ml) dry white wine
1 onion
4 ripe tomatoes
1 tablespoon olive oil
1 tablespoon flour
Bouquet garni
Freshly-ground black pepper
Pinch powdered saffron
2 tablespoons finely-chopped parsley

Scrub the mussels under cold running water, discarding any that do not close tightly when tapped. Pull off the wiry 'beards' sticking out of the shells.

Peel and chop the shallots. Place the mussels and chopped shallots in a large heavy pan. Pour over the white wine and cook over a high heat, shaking the pan, for about three minutes or until the mussels have opened. Strain off the cooking liquid through a fine sieve, leave the mussels to cool until you can handle them and then pull off the top parts of the shells and arrange the mussels in the half shell in a large, shallow dish.

Peel and finely chop the onion. Pour boiling water over the tomatoes and leave them to stand for 2 minutes. Slide off the skin, remove the core and seeds and chop the flesh.

Heat the olive oil in a saucepan, add the onion and cook over a low heat until the onion is just transparent. Add the flour and mix well. Gradually blend in the liquid in which the mussels were cooked, stirring continually until the sauce comes to the boil and is smooth. Add the tomatoes, bouquet garni and a good seasoning of pepper and the saffron and cook gently for 8 minutes. Pour the sauce over the mussels, sprinkle with parsley and serve at once.

Tomasine's Mussel Dish

Mussels in a delicately-flavoured creamy sauce with a hint of curry. A rich first course, but very good indeed.

Serves 4

2 quarts (2 litres) mussels
3 shallots or 1 large onion
3 sprigs parsley
3 oz (75 g) butter
1 bay leaf
2½ fl oz (75 ml) white wine
¼ pint (150 ml) water
1 tablespoon flour
2 teaspoons curry powder
¼ pint (150 ml) double cream

Scrub the mussels under cold running water and pull off the wiry 'beards' poking out from the shells. Discard any mussels that do not close tight shut when tapped. Peel and finely chop the shallots. Chop the parsley.

Melt 2 oz (50 g) of the butter in a large heavy pan. Add the shallots and cook over a low heat until soft and transparent. Add the parsley, bay leaf, mussels, white wine and water. Cover the pan, increase the heat and cook for about 3 minutes, shaking the pan every now and then, until all the mussels have opened. Strain off the liquid and leave the mussels to cool.

Remove the mussels from their shells.

Melt remaining butter in a saucepan. Add the flour and curry powder and mix well. Gradually add ½ pint (275 ml) of the cooking liquid, stirring continually over a medium high heat until the sauce comes to the boil and is thick and smooth. Add the cream and mussels, heat through and serve at once.

Pickled Mussels

> 1½ pints (875 ml) malt vinegar
> 1 oz (25 g) pickling spice (obtainable from Boots)
> 6 pints (3½ litres) mussels
> 1 teaspoon salt
> 1 pint (575 ml) water

Combine the vinegar and spices and boil for 15 minutes. Strain and cool. Scrub the mussels with a brush (a wire one is easier, or you can use a sharp knife) to remove any mud, barnacles, etc. Throw them into a large pan containing boiling salted water and boil over a high heat until the mussels have all opened. Leave until cool enough to handle.

Discard any mussels that do not open during the cooking time. Carefully pull out the wiry 'beards' protruding from the mussels and gently pull them from their shells. As you take each cleaned mussel from its shell put it in the cold, spiced vinegar.

Leave the mussels to marinade and then strain off excess vinegar before serving mussels chilled, with a salad.

Note: Cockles can be pickled in the same way.

CRAYFISH

Crayfish were once a popular delicacy in England. They were eaten with a 'salat', in a white sauce or as a soup, but I firmly maintain that they are best of all boiled, *au naturel*, and served cold.

Plunge the live crayfish into a large pan of boiling water to which a little olive oil and some salt and fresh dill have been added. As soon as they have turned from grey to bright pink, remove them from the water and leave to cool.

Serve the crayfish with home-made mayonnaise; crack the claws, pull off the head, sucking it to pull out the goodness, and peel the shell from the body.

Buttered and Creamed Lobsters

With lobsters being the price they are these days I don't really recommend eating them in any other but the simplest of ways. If you like your food rich and spicy then it is really more sensible to use a more inexpensive shellfish like crab (or crayfish if you can get it) to make a thermidor or other extravagant dish. In this recipe the lobster is served hot and just subtly blended with butter, cream and seasonings.

Serves 4

2 medium, lobsters cooked
2½ oz (65 g) butter
½ teaspoon made English mustard
Salt and freshly-ground black pepper
Pinch cayenne pepper
2½ fl oz (75 ml) double cream
Browned breadcrumbs

Using a stout sharp-pointed knife, cut through the lobster's shell along the length of the back and separate the lobster into halves. Remove and discard the gritty stomach sac from the head and the thin black line of intestine running through the body. Pull off the claws, crack them and pull out all the meat from inside. Remove all the flesh from the body and cut into 1 in (2½-cm) pieces.

Melt 1½ oz (40 g) butter in a saucepan. Add the mustard and mix in the lobster meat. Season with salt, pepper and a pinch of cayenne and cook over a medium heat, stirring lightly, until the meat is coated with seasoned butter. Mix in the cream, remove from the heat and fill the shells with the lobster meat.

Sprinkle over enough breadcrumbs to make a thin layer.

Melt the remaining butter, dribble it over the lobster halves and grill under a medium high heat until the crumbs are crisp and the lobster hot through.

Lobster Salad

This must surely be one of the most delicious things to eat on a hot day with the sun shining and a bottle of well-chilled white wine to go with it.

Serves 4

1 onion
½ lemon
2 2-lb (900-g) lobsters (preferably bought alive)
2 tablespoons olive oil
Bouquet garni
1 lettuce
2 large firm and ripe tomatoes
2 spring onions
½ cucumber

For an uncooked lobster: Peel and slice the onion and slice the half lemon. Place the lobsters in a large saucepan with the onion slices and lemon, add the olive oil and bouquet garni, cover with cold water and bring very slowly to the boil over a low heat. As soon as the water begins to bubble, remove it from the heat and leave to cool in a cold place. Just bringing the water to the boil is enough to cook the lobsters while keeping them moist and succulent.

Lay the lobsters on their stomachs and using a stout sharp-pointed knife, cut through the shell down the length of the back. Separate the halves and remove and discard the gritty stomach sac from the head and the thin black line of intestine running down the length of the body.

Wash and dry the lettuce leaves and shred roughly with the fingers to prevent bruising. Scald the tomatoes, slide off the skins and slice thinly. Chop the spring onions. Skin and thinly slice the cucumber.

Arrange a bed of lettuce leaves on four large plates. Place the lobsters on top and surround them with the slices of tomato and cucumber. Sprinkle over the spring onions and serve chilled with home-made mayonnaise.

CRAB

Cook raw crabs in boiling water for about 15 minutes to the pound. Test crabs for weight when you buy them. They should be surprisingly heavy for their size. Light crabs will mean poor flesh and sometimes that they have been left standing around and the flesh inside has dried up.

Keep an eye out, in some markets, for crab legs and claws which, although a tedious job to deal with, provide an extremely inexpensive form of shellfish. Watch out, if you buy fresh prepared crabmeat, that you are not buying almost 100% brown meat instead of a fair mixture of brown and white.

To Dress Cooked Crabs

Allow a medium crab for two people.

1 crab
2 hard-boiled eggs
2 tablespoons finely-grated white breadcrumbs
2 tablespoons double cream
1 teaspoon mustard
Salt and freshly-ground black pepper

Remove the large claws and twist off the legs. Using the thumbs, press the shell upwards and remove. Scrape the brown meat from the inside of the shell. Reserve the shell to use as a serving dish. Remove the poisonous stomach sac, any green matter and the 'dead men's fingers' (white spongy fingers to each side of the body). Split the body of the crab in half and pick out the white meat – this is a process which needs patience and it may have to be broken in more than one place.

Remove the yolks of the eggs and chop the egg whites. Add the breadcrumbs to the brown meat with the cream and mustard, season with salt and pepper. Arrange the brown meat in a line down the centre of the crab shell, and the white meat on either side. Top the brown meat with the chopped egg whites and the white meat with the egg yolks rubbed through a coarse sieve.

Serve with brown bread and butter and a home-made mayonnaise.

Potato Croquettes with Crab

Serve this as a light lunch or supper dish or as a first course.

Serves 4

1½ lb (675 g) potatoes
2 egg yolks
½ oz (15 g) butter
2–4 tablespoons milk
2 oz (50 g) white crab meat
1 tablespoon finely-chopped parsley
Salt and freshly-ground black pepper
Pinch of cayenne
1 small egg, beaten
Browned breadcrumbs

Peel the potatoes and cook them in boiling salted water until just tender. Drain very well and then mash until smooth. Add the egg yolks, the butter and enough milk to make a thick, smooth consistency. Add the crab and parsley and season with salt, pepper and a pinch of cayenne. Leave in a refrigerator until well chilled.

Using floured hands, shape the potatoes into thick sausage shapes about 1½ in (4 cm) thick and 2 in (5 cm) long. Roll in beaten egg and coat all over with breadcrumbs. Fry the croquettes in a mixture of butter and oil until crisp and golden brown.

Serve the croquettes with the following sauce.

Sauce for Potato Croquettes with Crab

½ pint (275 ml) mayonnaise
1 tablespoon tomato ketchup
1 tablespoon finely-chopped chives
½ tablespoon chopped capers
Few drops Worcestershire sauce
2 tablespoons double cream

Combine all the ingredients and mix well.

Crab Pancakes

Serves 4

The pancakes:

4 oz (125 g) flour
Pinch salt
1 egg
½ pint (275 ml) milk
Olive oil

The filling:

1½ oz (40 g) butter
1 tablespoon flour
¼ pint (150 ml) milk
4 tablespoons white wine
Salt, freshly-ground black pepper and a pinch of
    cayenne
2 tablespoons double cream
3 oz (75 g) white crab meat
1 oz (25 g) peeled prawns
1 tablespoon chopped chives or spring onion tops
2 oz (50 g) grated Cheddar cheese

Combine the flour with a pinch of salt, the egg and ½ pint
(275 ml) of milk and beat with a rotary or electric whisk until

smooth. Leave to stand for 30 minutes. Heat a little olive oil in an omelette pan, swirling the oil around until it begins to smoke. Add about a tablespoon of pancake batter, swirling it around the pan until the bottom is coated with a thin film. Cook over a high heat for about 3 minutes until the pancake is lightly browned on the bottom and set firm. Turn over and brown the other side. Slide the pancake on to a plate and continue in the same way with the rest of the batter. Stack the pancakes, one on top of another, until all the batter has been used.

Melt the butter. Add the flour and gradually blend in $\frac{1}{4}$ pint (150 ml) milk, stirring continually over a medium high heat until the sauce is thick and smooth. Add the wine, season with salt and pepper and cayenne and cook over a low heat for 3 minutes. Stir in the cream and lightly mix in the crab meat, prawns and chopped chives or spring onion tops.

Spread the filling over the pancakes and roll them up neatly. Place the rolled pancakes in a lightly-buttered baking dish, sprinkle over the cheese and bake in a moderately hot oven (400° F, Reg 6) for about 10 minutes until the pancakes are hot through and the cheese has melted.

OYSTERS

At Port Navas on the Helford River in Cornwall, the Duchy own oyster beds and a small factory from which oysters are dispatched to London, to other parts of the country and even to Brittany. The beds are old and well tried and are said to have been there in Roman days; certainly conditions are ideal, for in bad winters when Colchester and Whitstable beds have been wiped out the Helford beds have survived well enough to be able to supply those stricken areas with young oysters for fattening.

Oyster Patties

On our frolics to the Duchy of Cornwall oyster beds at Port Navas, we often stop for a drink with Annie and Bekas Penrose in the lovely palladian house just west of Truro. Annie is a deliciously flamboyant character and the Penrose house is the epitome of hospitality, as warm and glowing in its ambience as in its decor. One of our greatest delights is when Annie makes oyster patties, light as a feather and with the subtlest of all tastes. Nothing has ever quite come up to that phrase 'melts in the mouth' as do those patties.

Patties, small tarts with a savoury filling, were once popular fare throughout the West Country, and they make a perfect first course to start off any special meal these days.

Serves 4

½ lb (225 g) plain flour
Pinch salt
3 oz (75 g) butter
1 oz (25 g) lard
1 teaspoon lemon juice
12 oysters, opened (these can be bought in tins)
2 egg yolks
¼ pint cream (150 ml)
Juice ½ lemon
1 tablespoon finely-chopped parsley
Freshly-ground black pepper

Put the flour in a bowl with a pinch of salt. Add the fats cut into small pieces and rub into the flour with the fingertips until the mixture resembles coarse breadcrumbs. Add the lemon juice and enough cold water to make a stiff dough. Turn on to a floured board and knead lightly until smooth. Chill the pastry for about 30 minutes before rolling out.

Roll out the pastry as thinly as possible and line twelve tartlet tins. Line each pastry case with foil and fill with dried beans. Bake the cases in a hot oven (425° F, Reg 7) for 5 minutes, then remove the foil and beans and bake for a further 10 minutes or until crisp and light golden in colour.

Boil the oysters with their liquid for 2 minutes. Then strain the liquid through a fine sieve into a clean pan. Bring the liquid to the boil and cook over a high heat until reduced by about half.

Remove the beards from the oysters and cut each one in half. Beat the egg yolks with the cream. Cook over a very low heat until the mixture begins to thicken, add the lemon juice, about 3 tablespoons of oyster liquor and the parsley. Season with pepper and mix in the oysters. Spoon the filling into the cases and serve at once.

Fried Oysters

This recipe can also be made with tinned oysters, which are good value. It makes a good first course, but the oysters must be served as soon as they are hot.

Serves 4

24 oysters
2 eggs, beaten
Browned breadcrumbs
Oil for frying
Wedges of lemon
Brown bread and butter

Coat the oysters in beaten egg and then roll them in breadcrumbs until they are well covered. Pour about 1½ in (4 cm) of cooking oil into a large frying pan and heat until smoking. Add the oysters and cook over a high heat for about 2 minutes only, until golden brown and crisp. Drain on kitchen paper and serve at once with wedges of lemon and slices of buttered brown bread.

SNAILS

The idea that snails could be eaten was introduced to the British by the Romans and the practice is still carried out in Somerset. In the famous Miner's Arms near Priddy snails are known as 'Wallfish' and the owner of this pub produces frozen and tinned packs to sell in London. They also boil their snails in cider and serve them in the restaurant with a sauce of cream cheese and herbs.

The texture of snails is more important than their taste and, to my mind, the best way to serve them is still in a traditionally French butter sauce of herbs and garlic with strong overtones of parsley. To keep the snails upright, press them into thick slices of white bread – the bread will also serve to capture the essential sauce and can be used to mop up the plate after the snails have been eaten.

The sauce also goes well with whelks (if you can buy them in their shells) and with oysters.

Butter Sauce for Snails, Whelks or Oysters

> 4 oz (125 g) softened butter
> 2 tablespoons finely-chopped parsley
> 2 cloves garlic
> Salt and freshly-ground black pepper
> 1 tablespoon finely-chopped chives
> 2 teaspoons lemon juice

Combine all the ingredients and mix well. Put drained snails into their shells, spread the butter over the top and heat the snails in a moderately hot oven (400° F, Reg 6) for about 15 minutes until the butter has melted and is boiling hot.

3

Cornish Pasties, the Taste of the West Country Complete Meals in a Package

Light parcels of mouthmelting pastry enclosing any number of varied ingredients, the perfect lunch, supper or picnic food with its ancient traditions hidden in the mists of Cornish tin-mining history.

'Pastry rolled out like a plate
Piled with "turmut[1], tates[2] and mate[3]"
Doubled up, and baked like fate,
That's a Cornish Pasty.' (Anon)

1 turnip   2 potatoes   3 meat, pronounced 'mert' by the Cornish

PASTIES are the secret of the Cornish, an ancient food with its origins hidden in time, a meal in a package invented for men folk to take to work, small enough to put into a large pocket yet substantial enough to keep a large man going for a long day.

Not long ago I was fortunate enough to be able to go down the South Crofty Mine at Camborne. For four hours Robin and I followed the Captain of the mine along the dark warmth of a maze of tunnels, watching men drilling with diamonds for tin, seeing others stripped to the waist preparing new ground for dynamiting or driving mini trains piled high with rocks. When break time came the men sat down, underground, lamps shining above dust-streaked faces, to drink their tea and unwrap the newspaper parcels in which their pasties were still warm, eating them in the traditional manner, holding them in their right hand and munching from one narrow end, not from the middle. Deep down below the surface of the earth I felt as if I might be living 200 years ago or more. Equipment had changed but very little else, and the food those men were eating was probably one of the most authentically British dishes still to be found in this country.

All the flavour of the ingredients is sealed in the pastry casing and moisture is provided by the juices of the filling. A good pasty doesn't crumble or come apart in your hands, but is firm and moist with the filling so tender it melts in your mouth.

A pasty, in English cooking terms, refers to ingredients, both sweet and savoury, encased in pastry but with the pastry being folded over the ingredients rather than shaped around a pie dish. Although pasties are considered to be very much the staple diet of the Cornish, they appear in many forms throughout the West Country. In Cornwall you will find pasties filled with any manner of ingredients (so much so that it is said that the devil never dared cross the Tamar River from Devonshire to Cornwall for fear of the Cornish women's habit of putting anything and everything into a pasty) and in Somerset you can still find such delights as 'Priddy Oggies', a mixture of cheese and pork.

Pasties, though, are basically Cornish, and a pride of the county. Having lived on the windswept gorse- and heather-clad hills of Bodmin Moor for seventeen years, I suppose it is not surprising that pasties, to me too, have become almost an obsession. A bad one fills me with disgust. I bridle when I see cafés and food stalls out of the county selling 'pasties' which have nothing in common with the light pastry casing and succulent, robustly-flavoured filling of the real thing. Meat pasties made out of beef and vegetables are the most commonly-found version of this dish and also the most abused. In a real pasty the meat must be cut, by hand, into minute slivers (shaved might be a better term for the cutting of the meat). The potatoes and turnip can be coarsely grated and the onion is chopped, but on no account should the meat be minced as that not only draws out the moisture from the meat but also ruins the texture of the filling.

Cornish Pasty

Serves 5

Pastry:

2 lb (900 g) self-raising flour
¾lb (350 g) margarine
¾ pint (425 ml) water

Filling:

1 lb (450 g) beef skirt (fat removed)
2 small onions
1 small turnip
1 lb (450 g) potatoes
2 lb (900 g) cooking apples
Salt and freshly-ground black pepper
1½ oz (40 g) butter
4 oz (125 g) sugar
1 small beaten egg

To make the pastry, sieve the flour into a large basin. Add the margarine, cut into small pieces, and cut it into the flour using two sharp knives. Continue to cut until the mixture resembles coarse breadcrumbs. Add the water, mix by hand until the mixture forms a firm dough, place in a polythene bag and chill for at least 20 minutes.

To prepare the filling, cut the beef into thin slivers using a sharp knife (some people mince their meat for pasties but this really does ruin the flavour). Peel and finely chop the onion. Peel and coarsely grate the turnip and the potato. Cover the potatoes and turnip with cold water until required.

Peel, core and thickly slice the apples and cover them with cold water until required.

Using a well-floured board roll out the pastry to ⅛ in (3 mm) thickness, large enough to cut into five circles using a 10 in (25 cm) plate as a guide. From the remaining dough, rolled out thinly, cut five triangles, roughly 3¼ in (8½ cm) on each side, for the dividing wall. Dip one edge of a dividing triangle in water and press it firmly across the centre of pastry circle. Repeat with remaining circles.

Place the meat, potato, turnip and onion on one side of the dividing layer and the apples on the other side (drain all the ingredients before placing on pastry). Season the savoury side of the pasties with salt and pepper mixed with a small knob of softened butter and flavour the other side with sugar. Bring the edges of the pastry together so that the dividing layer triangle forms a barrier through the centre, moisten all the edges well (no juice should be allowed to seep through from the savoury to the sweet side) and crimp the top edges of the pastry together to make a neat ridge. Make a small cross or other symbol on one end of the pastry to indicate the savoury end. Brush the pasties with beaten egg and bake in a moderately hot oven (400° F, Reg 6) for 20 minutes and then reduce the heat to very moderate (325° F, Reg 3) for a further 30–35 minutes until the meat is tender. (Make a small slit to test the filling.)

Leave to cool for 15 minutes before eating from your hands from the savoury end towards the pudding course.

If the pasties are to be taken on a picnic, wrap them in generous layers of newspaper and pack them tightly in a cardboard box; they will retain some of their heat for a considerable length of time.

Meat Pasties

Serves 4

Pastry:

12 oz (350 g) plain flour
¼ teaspoon salt
6 oz (175 g) margarine
1 small egg, beaten

Filling:

12 oz (350 g) chuck or blade steak or skirt
8 oz (225 g) potatoes
1 small piece turnip or swede
1 onion
Salt and pepper

To make the pastry, sieve the flour into a bowl with ¼ teaspoon salt. Add the margarine, cut into small pieces, and rub it into the flour with the fingertips until the mixture resembles coarse breadcrumbs. Add enough water (approximately 3 tablespoons) to make a stiff dough, kneading with your hands until the pastry is smooth. Put the pastry into a polythene bag and leave in a refrigerator for 30 minutes before rolling out.

To prepare the filling, use a sharp knife to scrape the meat into very small slivers (mincing destroys the texture of the meat and makes it inclined to dry out during cooking). Peel and coarsely grate the potato and turnip or swede. Peel and finely chop the onion.

Roll out the pastry on a well-floured board to about $\frac{1}{8}$ in (3 mm) thickness and cut into four circles 8 in (20 cm) in diameter. Divide the meat between the four circles and top with the potato, turnip and onion. Season generously with salt and pepper. Draw up the edges of the pastry circles to make a seam across the top, pinching the edges together firmly and then crimping them over with the fingertips to make a neat join.

Brush the pasties with beaten egg, place them on a baking sheet and bake in a hot oven (425° F, Reg 7) for 15 minutes. Lower the heat to moderate (325° F, Reg 3) and continue to bake for a further 25–30 minutes.

When the pasties are taken out of the oven, a small slit can be made in the top of each one and a little melted butter or cream can be poured in.

Lamb and Parsley Pasty

Use any lean lamb combined with a little lamb fat to prevent the meat drying. Make the pastry and prepare the pasties as for Meat Pasties (see page 81).

Serves 4

$\frac{1}{2}$ lb (225 g) lamb
1 large bunch parsley
1 onion

Salt and freshly-ground black pepper
1 oz (25 g) butter

Using a sharp knife, scrape the lamb into small slivers.
Remove the stalks of the parsley and very finely chop the
leaves. Peel and finely chop the onion. Place the lamb in the
centre of the four pastry circles and top with onion and
parsley. Season with salt and pepper, dot with butter and
finish as for Meat Pasties.

Eggy Pasties

One could call this version of a pasty 'breakfast in a pastry
package'. I add finely-chopped parsley to the pasties and
cook them for a little less than the normal time. Follow
directions for making pastry for pasties on page 81.

Serves 4

4 large rashers of streaky bacon, rind removed
4 eggs
2 tablespoons finely-chopped parsley
Salt and freshly-ground black pepper
1 oz (25 g) butter

Arrange each rasher on its edge in a circle in the centre of
each circle of pastry. Break the eggs one by one into a cup
and slide them into the centre of the bacon circles. Top with
finely-chopped parsley, season with salt and pepper and dot
with a little butter. Draw the edges of the pastry up together
and crimp edges very firmly. Brush pastry with a little egg
and bake in a hot oven (425° F, Reg 7) for 10 minutes, then
lower the heat to moderate (350° F, Reg 4) and continue to
bake for a further 20 minutes.
    Serve hot or warm.

Bacon and Herb Pasties

Follow directions for making pastry and for putting together the pasties on page 81.

Serves 4

1 bunch parsley
8 oz (225 g) spinach
8 oz (225 g) bacon
3 small shallots
1 egg, beaten

Finely chop the parsley, having removed the stalks. Wash and finely chop the spinach. Put the parsley and spinach into a bowl and cover with boiling water. Leave to stand for 30 minutes and then drain well, squeezing out all excess water.

Remove the rind from the bacon and chop the rashers into small pieces. Peel and finely chop the shallots.

Combine these ingredients and divide the filling between four pastry circles. Draw the edges together and crimp firmly, leaving a small hole in the centre of each pasty to pour in the beaten egg before closing tightly together.

Follow the directions for baking the pasties on page 82.

Mackerel Pasties

I only tried these when doing the research for this book. The practice of making them seems to have died out now, but years ago I believe they were popular in fishing villages when money was scarce and housewives had to make do on the fish their husbands brought home from the day's fishing.

Make the pastry and prepare the pasties in the same way as Meat Pasties (page 81).

Serves 4

4 small mackerel

1 bunch parsley
Salt and freshly-ground black pepper

Remove the heads and tails from the mackerel and clean the fish. Using a sharp knife remove the skin and bones from the fish and finely chop the flesh. Cut off the stalks from the parsley and finely chop the leaves.

Divide the mackerel and parsley between the four circles of pastry, top with finely-chopped parsley and season with salt and pepper. Finish and cook as for Meat Pasties.

Cornish Muggity Pie

This was a popular West Country pie in the far West Country during the Elizabethan and later eras. I haven't included the recipe because it was made from sheep's lights (lungs), with a generous portion of currants, brown sugar and parsley, all wrapped up in a pastry case. The sweetness of this dish would not, I feel, be appreciated by many people nowadays and sheep's lights, to be realistic, are not easy to find on a supermarket shelf. But I felt the dish should be mentioned, because it was, for a few hundred years, a well-known Cornish delicacy.

Tiddy Oggie

Things were very hard indeed when the tin mines closed in Cornwall. For the miners' wives, each day was a matter of trying to feed a family, often a large family, on next to nothing. Tiddy Oggies were for when things got to their lowest and pasties had to be made with a filling of potatoes, a smidgin of onion, seasoning and nothing else at all.

Priddy Oggie

In Somerset, things never got as bad as they did in Cornwall. The land was more rich and there were few mines to close;

nevertheless the economical pasty recipes spread eastwards and in Somerset they made their pasties by combining a few bits of pork with cheese for a savoury meal in a pastry casing. Make the pastry and prepare the pasties as for Meat Pasties (see page 81).

Serves 4

¾ lb (350 g) pork fillet
1 small rasher lean bacon
3 oz (75 g) grated Cheddar cheese
2 teaspoons finely-chopped parsley
Pinch dried sage
Salt and freshly-ground black pepper
1 egg, beaten
Deep fat for frying

Remove any skin from the pork fillet and very finely chop (not mince) the flesh. Very finely chop the bacon. Combine the pork, bacon, cheese, herbs and seasoning, add half the beaten egg and mix well.

Divide the filling into four and assemble the pasties as in meat pasties (see page 81). Brush over with beaten egg and bake the pasties in a moderate oven (350° F, Reg 4) for about 10 minutes until the pastry is firm but not browned or crisp. Deep fry the half-baked 'Oggies' in hot deep fat for a further 10–15 minutes until they are crisp and golden brown. Drain well on kitchen paper before serving.

Beef, Leek and Potato Pie

An economical pie using shin beef. Partly cook the beef first before putting on the pie crust to ensure that it is tender.

Serves 4

1 lb (450 g) shin beef
1½ lb (675 g) potatoes
4 leeks

1½ pints (875 ml) beef stock
Salt and freshly-ground black pepper
8 oz (225 g) plain flour
2 oz (50 g) lard
2 oz (50 g) suet
1 small egg, beaten

Cut the meat into small pieces. Peel the potatoes and cut them into 2 in (5 cm) cubes. Clean the leeks and cut each one in half lengthwise. Combine the meat and potatoes in a pie dish with the stock. Season with salt and pepper, cover with foil and cook in a slow oven (300° F, Reg 2) for 1½ hours.

Put the flour into a bowl and add a little salt. Rub the lard and suet into the flour with the fingertips until the mixture resembles coarse breadcrumbs. Add enough water to make a stiff dough and knead until firm. Roll out the pastry to about ¼ in (6 mm) thickness.

Place the leeks on top of the meat and potatoes, damp the edges of the pie dish, cover with the pastry and press the edges down firmly. Brush with beaten egg and bake in a hot oven (425° F, Reg 7) for 10 minutes then lower the heat to moderate (350° F, Reg 4) and continue to cook for a further 45 minutes.

Lamb Pie with New Potatoes

The habit of cooking meat with potatoes and then putting on a pie crust is one that has rather fallen off. Originally these pies were made to stretch meat as far as possible but, as people became more prosperous (and perhaps more figure conscious) it was considered wrong to incorporate both the starch of pastry and the starch of potatoes in the same dish. Now that meat has become so much more expensive perhaps the practice of meat and potato pies will come back into favour.

Serves 6

8 oz (225 g) flour
2 oz (50 g) butter
2 oz (50 g) lard
Iced water
3 lb (1·4 kg) leg spring lamb
Flour
Salt and freshly-ground black pepper
1½ lb (675 g) small new potatoes
1 large onion
Stock (or water and stock cube)
2 tablespoons finely-chopped mint

Sieve 8 oz (225 g) flour with a little salt into a bowl. Add the fats cut into small pieces and rub into the flour with fingertips until the mixture resembles coarse breadcrumbs. Add just enough iced water to make a firm dough. Turn the dough on to a floured board and knead lightly until smooth. Leave it to chill in the refrigerator until required.

Cut the meat off the bones and then into 1-in (2½-cm) pieces (the bones can be used to make a good home-made stock for this or another dish). Roll the meat in flour seasoned with salt and pepper. Scrape the potatoes. Peel and finely chop the onion.

Place the meat and onion in a pie dish and pour over enough stock to cover. Cover and cook in a moderate oven (350° F, Reg 4) for 1–1½ hours until the meat is tender.

Add the potatoes and the mint (you may need to add a little more stock too but the pie should not be too liquid) and mix to incorporate the ingredients.

Roll the pastry out thinly and cut thin strips to go round the edge of the pie dish. Dampen the strips of pastry and press them firmly around the edge of the dish. Cover with a pastry lid, pressing the edges firmly. Cut an air vent in the top and bake the pie in a moderately hot oven (375° F, Reg 5) for 30 minutes, by which time the top should be golden brown and the potatoes should be tender and flavoured with the meat juices.

Serve with young peas and perhaps baby carrot thinnings from the vegetable garden.

Lambs' Tail Pie

An old Dorsetshire recipe for coping with lambs' tails.

Serves 6

2 lb (900 g) lambs' tails
½ lb (225 g) lard
1 lb (450 g) self-raising flour
Salt and freshly-ground black pepper
Ice-cold water
2 large onions
1½ pints (875 ml) stock
4 hard-boiled eggs
3 tablespoons finely-chopped parsley
½ teaspoon finely-chopped thyme
½ teaspoon finely-chopped marjoram
5 rashers streaky bacon
1 egg, beaten

Put the tails into a large bowl or bucket and sprinkle over a handful of salt. Pour over enough boiling water to cover and leave for 20 minutes. Using a sharp pointed knife cut down the length of the tail through the skin and neatly peel off the skin and wool, leaving the clean, skinned tails. Drop each tail into cold salted water as soon as it is cleaned.

Rub the lard into the flour and a pinch of salt until the lard is the size of peas and each piece is well coated with flour. Add enough ice-cold water to make a firm dough (handle it as little as possible) and chill the pastry in a refrigerator for at least 30 minutes before rolling out.

Peel and chop the onions. Drain the tails, chop them into

2-in (5-cm) lengths and combine with the onions in a large saucepan. Add enough stock to cover and bring to the boil, cover and simmer for 1½–2 hours until the tails are tender. Strain off the stock.

Slice the hard-boiled eggs. Roll the lambs' tails in chopped parsley, thyme and marjoram and arrange half of them in a lightly-greased pie dish. Put the hard-boiled eggs, and the bacon, with rinds removed and rashers cut into small pieces, over the tails and top with the remaining tails. Season the layers with salt and pepper and pour over just enough of the stock to cover.

Roll out the pastry, cover the pie, dampening the edge of the pie dish and pressing the pastry down firmly. Brush with beaten egg. Bake the pie in a hot oven (425° F, Reg 7) for 10 minutes, then lower the heat to moderate (350° F, Reg 4) and continue to cook for a further 15 minutes until the pastry is golden brown and the pie is hot through.

Leave the pie to cool overnight and serve cold with a new potato and a green or mixed salad.

Devonshire Squab Pie

Squab really applies to pigeons, young, plump and tender and not long out of their nests. When pigeons were hard to find, mutton and then lamb were used instead for this traditional Devonshire pie that combines meat with cider, leeks and apples.

Serves 6

8 oz (225 g) plain flour
Salt and freshly-ground black pepper
2 oz (50 g) butter
2 oz (50 g) lard
6 lamb cutlets from the best end of neck
4 cooking apples
6 medium leeks
Pinch allspice

Pinch nutmeg
1½ tablespoons sugar
About ½ pint (275 ml) medium dry cider

Sieve the flour into a bowl with a little salt. Cut in the fat
with two knives and then rub into the flour with your fingertips, working until the mixture resembles coarse breadcrumbs.
Add enough water to make a stiff dough, and then knead on
a floured board until the pastry is smooth and pliable.
Cover with a cloth and chill in a refrigerator for 30 minutes
before rolling out.

Trim off excess fat from the cutlets. Peel, core and slice the
apples; clean and roughly chop the leeks. Arrange the
cutlets in a lightly-greased pie dish, season with salt and
pepper, and cover with alternate layers of apple and leeks,
seasoning each layer and adding a little allspice, ground
nutmeg and the sugar. Pour over enough cider to just cover
the ingredients.

Roll out the pastry to about ¼ in (6 mm) thick and cover
the dish, damping the edges of the pastry and pressing them
down firmly on the edge of the pie dish. Decorate with
pastry trimming cut into the shape of leaves, brush with
milk and cut an air vent in the centre. Bake in a moderately
hot oven (400° F, Reg 6) for 10 minutes then cover with foil
or a piece of damp greaseproof paper and continue to cook
in a warm oven (300° F, Reg 2) for a further 1 hour and 15
minutes.

Note: As with all West Country pies you can slide some
double or clotted cream into the squab pie under the pastry
crust just before you serve it.

Economical Pork and Apple Pie

Serves 4

1¼ lb (575 g) lean pork
4 cooking apples

1 medium onion
¾ lb (350 g) good pork sausage meat
2 oz (50 g) fresh white breadcrumbs
1 teaspoon lemon peel
4 leaves sage
Salt and freshly-ground black pepper
Pinch of ground nutmeg and allspice
1½ oz (40 g) butter
½ pint (275 ml) dry cider
8 oz (225 g) plain flour
2 oz (50 g) lard
2 oz (50 g) butter
Small egg, beaten

Cut the pork into small dice; peel, core and slice the apples. Peel and finely chop the onion.

Combine the sausage meat, breadcrumbs, lemon peel, sage and onion, mix well and season with salt, pepper and a pinch of ground nutmeg and allspice. Arrange half the pork in a pie dish. Season with salt and pepper and cover with half the apple slices and the sausage meat. Dot with 1½ oz (40 g) of butter and fill with the remaining apples and pork. Pour over the cider.

Put the flour into a bowl with a pinch of salt and rub in the fats with the fingertips until the mixture resembles fine breadcrumbs. Add enough cold water to make a stiff dough, turn out on to a floured board and knead until smooth. Roll out to just under ¼ in (6 mm) thick and cover the pie, damping edges and pressing down firmly. Cut an air vent in the middle and brush with beaten egg.

Bake in a hot oven (425° F, Reg 7) for 10 minutes, reduce heat to moderately hot (350° F, Reg 4) and continue to cook for a further 1½ hours.

Meat and Giblet Pie

Serves 4–6

Giblets of 2 chickens (gizzards, necks, hearts and livers)
1 onion
20 peppercorns
2 blades mace
Salt and freshly-ground black pepper
A bouquet garni
1 lb (450 g) rump steak
8 oz (225 g) plain flour
2 oz (50 g) lard
2 oz (50 g) suet
1 small egg, beaten

Place the necks, gizzards and hearts in a saucepan. Add the onion, washed but not peeled and cut into quarters, the peppercorns, mace, $\frac{1}{2}$ teaspoon salt and a bouquet garni. Cover with 3 pints ($1\frac{1}{2}$ litres) water, bring to the boil, skim off any scum that rises to the surface and simmer for about 45 minutes or until the gizzards are tender. Strain off the liquid and remove the peppercorns and bouquet garni. Cut off the flesh from the neck bones and chop the gizzards and hearts.

Cut the chicken livers into small pieces. Cut the rump steak into 1-in ($2\frac{1}{2}$-cm) cubes and place it in the bottom of a pie dish. Top with the giblets and the liver and season with a little salt and pepper. Pour over enough of the strained stock to cover the ingredients.

Sift the flour into a bowl and add a little salt. Rub in the lard and suet with the fingertips until the mixture resembles coarse breadcrumbs. Add enough water to make a stiff dough and knead until smooth and firm. Roll out the pastry to about $\frac{1}{4}$ in (6 mm) thick. Damp the edges of the pie dish. Cover with the pastry, pressing the edges down firmly, and brush the top with beaten egg. Bake the pie in a hot oven

(425° F, Reg 7) for 10 minutes and then reduce the heat to moderate (350° F, Reg 4) for a further hour.

Chicken Split Pie

An almost miraculous way to make a chicken stretch to incredible lengths. Any leftovers can be used to make the base of a nourishing chicken soup.

Serves 8

Filling:

4 large carrots
3 onions
3 stalks celery
4 cloves garlic
1 large bunch parsley
1 large roasting chicken
3 tablespoons oatmeal
1 teaspoon ground saffron
Salt and freshly-ground black pepper

Stock:

Chicken neck, skin and carcass
1 chicken stock cube
Parsley stalks and Vegetable peelings

Topping:

8 oz (225 g) plain flour
1 teaspoon baking powder
1½ oz (40g) margarine
1 teaspoon dry mustard
Salt
4 oz (125 g) cottage cheese
Scant ¼ pint (125 ml) milk

Wash and peel the carrots, reserving the peelings, and

roughly chop. Skin the onions, reserving the skins and roughly chop. Remove and reserve the leaves of the celery and roughly chop the stalks. Peel and finely chop the garlic cloves. Remove the stalks from the parsley and finely chop the leaves.

Remove any tough skin from the chicken. Cut off the legs and divide the drumsticks from the thighs. Chop each joint in half with a meat cleaver. Cut off the wings and chop through the joints. Slice the breast meat from the chicken and cut into 1-in (2½-cm) cubes. Using a small sharp knife remove all remaining meat from the carcass. Cut the liver, heart and gizzard into small pieces.

Combine the oatmeal with the saffron, season with salt and pepper, add all the chicken meat and mix well.

Make a rich chicken stock from the chicken neck, skin, carcass and stock cube with the parsley stalks and vegetable peelings.

Pack the chicken meat in a lightly-greased pie dish with the chopped vegetables and parsley. Pour over enough chicken stock to cover.

Put the flour into a bowl and add baking powder, the margarine, mustard and salt. Cut the margarine and cottage cheese into the flour, using two sharp knives, until it is the size of small peas. Rub the mixture with the fingertips until it resembles coarse breadcrumbs and bind with enough milk to make a firm smooth dough. Roll out the dough on a floured board to a sausage shape about 2 in (5 cm) across and cut into ½ in (1 cm) thick slices. Press the slices into rough circles and spread them over the pie in overlapping circles. Brush the slices with a little milk and bake in a moderate oven (350° F, Reg 4) for 1 hour.

Rabbit Pie

Serves 4

Pastry:

6 oz (175 g) plain flour
Salt
2 oz (50 g) butter
1 oz (25 g) lard

Filling:

1 rabbit, jointed
Flour
Salt and freshly-ground black pepper
Pinch cayenne
2 large onions
8 oz (225 g) lean ham
2 oz (50 g) butter
2 bay leaves
Pinch finely-chopped sage and thyme
2 tablespoons finely-chopped parsley
1½ pints (875 ml) chicken stock

First make the pastry. Put the flour in a bowl with a pinch of salt. Add the butter and lard cut into small pieces. Rub the fats into the flour with the fingertips until the mixture resembles fine breadcrumbs. Add enough water to make a firm dough, turn on to a floured board and knead lightly until smooth. Cover the pastry with a cloth and chill in a refrigerator while making the filling.

Roll the rabbit joints in flour seasoned with salt, pepper and a pinch of cayenne. Peel and chop the onions. Cut the ham into thin, matchstick strips.

Melt the butter in a heavy frying pan. Add the onions and cook over a low heat until soft and transparent. Remove the onions with a slotted spoon, add the rabbit joints to the juices in the pan and cook over a high heat until lightly browned on all sides. Arrange the rabbit joints, onions and ham in a pie dish, add bay leaves and sprinkle over the herbs. Pour over the stock.

Roll out the pastry to about $\frac{1}{4}$ in (6 mm) thick. Damp the edges of the pie dish, cover with the pastry and press the edges firmly to the pie dish. Cut an air vent in the centre of the pie and bake in a moderately hot oven (400° F, Reg 6) for 10 minutes, then lower the heat to moderate (350° F, Reg 4) and continue to cook for a further 40 minutes, covering the top of the pie with a piece of greaseproof paper if it becomes too brown.

Cheese and Potato Pie

A satisfying lunch or supper dish that only needs the accompaniment of a salad or green vegetable.

Serves 4

1½ lb (675 g) potatoes
4 tablespoons top of the milk
1 egg, beaten
1 teaspoon made English mustard
6 oz (175 g) grated cheese
Salt and white pepper
2 tablespoons finely-chopped parsley
3 large tomatoes
1 oz (25 g) melted butter

Peel and roughly chop the potatoes and cook them until tender in lightly-salted water. Mash with the milk, egg, mustard and two-thirds of the cheese. Season with salt and pepper, mix in the parsley and spread in a lightly-greased baking dish.

Thinly slice the tomatoes and spread them evenly over the top of the potatoes. Season with a little salt and pepper and sprinkle over the remaining cheese. Dribble over the melted butter and bake in a moderately hot oven (400° F,

Reg 6) for about 20 minutes until golden brown and hot through.

Shabra Chipple and Bacon Flan

Shabra is an old Cornish farmhouse name. In this recipe the chipples (spring onions) are sliced lengthwise and used like leeks. Cream cheese added to the eggs gives a smooth texture and an extremely good flavour. It makes a perfect picnic dish.

Serves 4–6

Pastry:

6 oz (175 g) plain flour
Pinch salt
2 oz (50 g) butter
1 oz (25 g) lard

Filling:

4 rashers streaky bacon
1 tablespoon dripping or lard
6 chipples or spring onions
4 eggs
3 oz (75 g) cream cheese
2 tablespoons finely-chopped parsley
Salt and freshly-ground black pepper

Sieve the flour and salt into a bowl. Add the butter and lard cut into small pieces and cut into the flour using two knives. Rub the fat into the flour with the fingertips until the mixture resembles coarse breadcrumbs and work in enough cold water to make a firm dough. Knead until smooth, turn on to a floured board, roll out and use to line a 9-in (23-cm) flan case. Press foil over the pastry and bake for 10 minutes in a moderately hot oven (400° F, Reg 6). Lower heat to moderate (350° F, Reg 4), remove foil and bake the case 'blind' for a further 10 minutes. Leave to cool.

Remove rind from the bacon and roughly chop the rashers. Heat the dripping or lard in a frying pan, add the bacon pieces and the rinds and cook over a moderate heat for 5 minutes. Discard rinds and lift out bacon with a slotted spoon. Arrange bacon in the flan case.

Add the chipples to the juices in the pan and cook over a low heat until soft and transparent. Drain off excess fat and arrange chipples over the bacon.

Beat the eggs with the cream cheese (a rotary whisk is best for this) until the mixture is smooth. Mix in the parsley and season fairly generously with salt and pepper.

Pour the egg mixture over the bacon and chipples and bake in a moderately hot oven (350° F, Reg 4) for 20–30 minutes or until eggs are just set. (Cover with foil if the edges of the pastry tend to get too brown.)

Serve hot or cold.

Tregill Farm Pie

I have had this pie with both home-made and commercial sausage meat, and there is no doubt at all in my mind which is best – home-made sausage meat flavoured with fresh herbs wins every time. It may be a bit more expensive but it's well worth the extra cost.

Serves 6

6 oz (175 g) lean pork
6 oz (175 g) fat pork
2 oz (50 g) fresh white breadcrumbs
Milk
$\frac{1}{2}$ teaspoon mixed very finely-chopped sage and thyme
$\frac{1}{2}$ teaspoon finely-grated lemon rind
Juice of $\frac{1}{2}$ lemon
Salt and freshly-ground black pepper

2 cooking apples
3 large onions
3 large tomatoes
6 very thin rashers streaky bacon, rind removed
2 lb (900 g) mashed potatoes
1 oz (25 g) grated cheese
1 oz (25 g) butter

Mince the pork through the fine blades of a mincing machine. Soak the breadcrumbs in a little milk until soft. Add the softened breadcrumbs to the meat with the herbs, lemon rind and lemon juice, season with salt and pepper and mix well.

Peel, core and thinly slice the apples. Peel and thinly slice the onions and divide into rings. Scald the tomatoes, then peel off the skins and cut into thick slices.

Arrange the sausage meat in the bottom of a fireproof serving dish. Spread the onion rings on top and cover with the bacon rashers, apple and tomato slices. Season with salt and pepper. Cover the ingredients with the mashed potato and sprinkle over the grated cheese. Dot with the butter and bake in a moderate oven (350° F, Reg 4) for 1 hour and 15 minutes.

Salsify or Scorzonera Pie

Salsify, rightly called 'the oyster of the earth' is one of the most delicious vegetables in the world. Scorzonera, its cousin, is even better, although it's an ugly thing to look at. Once the black skin has been stripped off, the white inside root has a delicacy of flavour that is very special indeed.

This pie makes a good meal if it is served with crispy fried bacon and grilled tomatoes.

Serves 4

1 lb (450 g) salsify or scorzonera
1 lb (450 g) potatoes

2 oz (50 g) butter
2½ fl oz (75 ml) double cream
Salt and freshly-ground black pepper
2 tablespoons flour
¼ pint (150 ml) milk
Pinch nutmeg

Wash the salsify or scorzonera roots and cook them in boiling salted water until just tender. Drain and, as soon as they are cool enough to handle, strip off the skins. Cut the roots into 1-in (2½-cm) long pieces.

Boil the potatoes in salted water until tender and drain well. Mash the potatoes with ½ oz (15 g) of butter and 2 tablespoons of the cream and season with salt and pepper.

Melt the remaining butter in a saucepan, add the flour and mix well. Gradually blend in the milk, stirring continually over a medium high heat until the sauce is thick and smooth. Season with salt, pepper and a pinch of nutmeg, mix in the salsify or scorzonera and turn into a pie dish. Top with the mashed potato and bake in a moderately hot oven (400° F, Reg 6) for about 20 minutes until the pie is hot through and the top golden brown.

Bacon, Onion and Cheese Pie

Serves 4–6

12 oz (350 g) plain flour
1 teaspoon salt
4 oz (125 g) butter
4 oz (125 g) lard
Iced water
6 thin rashers streaky bacon
1 large Spanish onion
4 oz (125 g) grated Cheddar cheese
Salt and freshly-ground black pepper
1 small egg, beaten

First make the pastry: put the flour into a bowl with the salt. Add the fats and rub them in with the fingertips until the mixture resembles fine breadcrumbs. Add enough water to make a firm dough. Turn on to a floured board and knead until smooth. Roll out to $\frac{1}{8}$ in (3 mm) thick, turn both sides to the centre and roll again. Repeat folding and rolling process once more then roll up tightly, cover with a cloth and refrigerate until ready to use.

Remove the rinds from the bacon rashers and chop the flesh. Peel and thinly slice the onion and divide into rings. Roll out two-thirds of the pastry and line a fairly shallow pie dish. Place half the cheese in the bottom of the dish, cover with the onion and then with the bacon and top with remaining cheese. Season with salt and pepper and top with the remaining pastry rolled out to just about $\frac{1}{8}$ in (3 mm) thick, damping edges and pressing down firmly. Brush with beaten egg and bake in a hot oven (425° F, Reg 7) for 15 minutes, then lower heat and continue to bake in a moderate oven (350° F, Reg 4) for a further hour. (Cover the top of the pie with a sheet of dampened greaseproof paper if it begins to get too brown.)

Dartmoor Fidget Pie

Cider provides the liquid for this pie with an attractively-shaped pastry topping that exposes some of the filling.

Serves 4

1 lb (450 g) rashers streaky bacon
2 medium onions
1 lb (450 g) cooking apples
Salt and freshly-ground black pepper
$\frac{1}{2}$ pint (275 ml) cider
8 oz (225 g) plain flour
4 oz (125 g) butter or margarine
Iced water
1 small egg, beaten

Cut off the rinds from the bacon and cut the rashers into small dice. Peel and chop the onions; peel, core and dice the apples. Combine the bacon, onion and apple and put into a lightly-greased pie dish. Season with salt and pepper and pour over the cider.

Put the flour into a bowl with a pinch of salt. Cut in the butter with two knives and rub in with the fingertips until the mixture resembles coarse breadcrumbs. Add enough iced water to make a stiff dough. Turn on to a floured board and knead until firm and smooth. Roll out the pastry to about $\frac{1}{8}$ in (3 mm) thick. Damp the edge of the pie dish and cover with the pastry, press it firmly to the dish and trim off the edges. Make a cross in the centre, each slit about 6 in (15 cm) long and carefully fold back each triangle towards the edges of the pie.

Cut the pastry trimmings into crescent shapes. Press these around the outer edge of the pie and brush the whole of the pastry top with beaten egg.

Bake the pie in a moderately hot oven (400° F, Reg 6) for 20 minutes, then lower the heat and bake for a further 30 minutes in a moderate oven (350° F, Reg 4).

Leeky or Likky Pie

Another of those frugal dishes dating from when times were hard and there was no spare money for meat meals.

Serves 4

8 oz (225 g) plain flour
Salt
2 oz (50 g) lard
2 oz (50 g) butter
Iced water
12 large leeks
8 oz (225 g) bacon pieces
Salt and freshly-ground black pepper
$\frac{1}{4}$ pint (150 ml) gravy or rich stock

2 eggs
½ pint (275 ml) double cream

First make the pastry. Put the flour and salt into a bowl, add the fats, cut into small pieces, and rub into the flour with the fingertips. Add enough water to make a stiff dough, turn on to a floured board and knead until smooth and elastic.

Clean and cut the leeks into 1-in (2½-cm) pieces. Parboil the leeks in boiling salted water for 10 minutes and drain really well. Remove the rinds from the bacon and cut bacon into small pieces. Arrange layers of bacon and leeks in a lightly-greased pie dish, season each layer with a little salt and plenty of pepper and pour over the gravy or stock. Cover with the pastry – damp the edge of the dish and press it on firmly. Brush with a little milk and bake in a moderate oven (350° F, Reg 4) for 35–40 minutes.

Carefully remove the crust by sliding a knife around the edge and spoon out the liquid from the dish (this can be used for soup or gravy at another time). Beat the eggs with the cream, pour over the ingredients of the pie and return to the oven for 5 minutes.

Codling Pye

Although this is a delightfully simple and homely dish, I find it tastes so appealing that I have served small quantities of the mixture in ramekin dishes as a starter for a smart dinner party on a cold winter's evening.

Serves 4

1 lb (450 g) cod
2 oz (50 g) butter
2 oz (50 g) flour
¾ pint (425 ml) milk
8 oz (225 g) mashed potatoes
2 tablespoons finely-chopped parsley

Salt and cayenne pepper
2 oz (50 g) grated Cheddar cheese

Steam the fish over boiling water until it is tender (about 20 minutes). Leave until cool enough to handle, then remove any bones and skin and flake the flesh with a fork.

Melt the butter in a large saucepan. Add the flour and mix well; gradually blend in the milk, stirring continually over a medium high heat until the sauce comes to the boil and is thick and smooth. Remove from the heat and beat in the mashed potato. Add the parsley, season with salt and a little cayenne and mix well. Fold in the fish with a fork, mixing just enough to incorporate all the ingredients.

Put the mixture into a lightly-buttered baking dish, sprinkle over the cheese and bake in a moderately hot oven (375° F, Reg 5) until the top is bubbling and golden brown.

Note: Lightly butter the steamer before adding the fish to prevent it sticking to the pan as it tends to do.

4

Succulent Meat Dishes and Frugal Leftovers Made with Flair

Top-quality beef, lamb and pork are all raised in the West Country. Recipes include many meat dishes that are well tried in Cornwall, Devon, Somerset and Wiltshire and as good now as they ever were. Country women know how to make ends meet and leftovers are put to delicious advantage.

A GOOD STOCK can form the basis of a very good sauce. Gravy is good too, so don't throw away any leftover gravy when you next serve some with a roast joint or poultry – in this you have the ready made basis of many sauces. The fat poured from a pan after roasting meat or poultry will also yield a good proportion of meat drippings. These will settle in the bottom of a basin and form a jellied substance with the fat rising to the surface and making a solid mass that can be easily scraped off once the fat is cold.

Cucumber Sauce

The soft texture and delicate flavour of the cucumber is one that used to be used frequently to make a sauce to accompany roast lamb or pork. Try this recipe when cucumbers are cheap or available home-grown.

    1 large cucumber
    1 oz (25 g) butter
    Salt and freshly-ground black pepper
    Little ground nutmeg
    ½ pint (275 ml) gravy, meat drippings or stock

Peel the cucumber and cut into ½-in (1-cm) square dice. Melt the butter in a saucepan, add the cucumber, season with salt, pepper and a little nutmeg and cook, shaking the pan, until lightly browned. Pour over the gravy or stock and cook over a low heat for 15 minutes.

Note: If stock is used for this sauce it may turn out to be rather on the thin side. Rectify this by stirring in a little flour to the cucumber after it has been browned and gradually blend in the stock, stirring continually until the sauce is thickened and smooth. Test for seasoning before serving the sauce.

Mushroom Sauce

Use small button mushrooms for this sauce as the larger caps tend to discolour badly.

    1 onion
    4 cloves
    $\frac{1}{4}$ pint (150 ml) chicken (or water and stock cube)
    $\frac{1}{4}$ pint (150 ml) milk
    2 bay leaves
    4 oz (125 g) firm button mushrooms
    $1\frac{1}{2}$ oz (40 g) butter
    1 oz (25 g) flour
    Salt and freshly-ground black pepper
    1 teaspoon mushroom ketchup
    1 tablespoon cream

Peel the onion and stick the cloves into it. Combine the stock, milk, onion and bay leaves in a saucepan, bring to the boil and simmer for 15 minutes. Strain the liquid.

Chop the mushrooms. Melt $\frac{1}{2}$ oz (15 g) of butter in a small pan, add the mushrooms and cook over a very low heat, stirring every now and then, until the butter has all been absorbed.

Melt the remaining butter, add the flour and mix well. Gradually blend in the strained liquid stirring continually over a medium heat until the sauce is thick and smooth. Mix in the mushrooms, season with salt and pepper, add the mushroom ketchup and blend in the cream just before serving.

Mushroom Sauce with Ham

This makes a good topping for buttered toast to serve as a light supper or lunch dish.

Add 2 oz (50 g) of chopped ham and a little chopped parsley to the sauce, heat through and spread on hot buttered toast. Serve at once.

Cider Sauce

Everyone has heard of Cumberland sauce to serve with hot or cold boiled ham or tongue; this is a less expensive but equally good version of that mellow fruity sauce, invented by the chef of the Taunton Cider Company. It keeps well and is particularly good if it is made with a home-made crab apple jelly.

½ pint (275 ml) Taunton Autumn Gold cider
6 oz (175 g) home-made crab apple jelly or redcurrant jelly
Thinly-pared rind and juice of 1 orange
Juice ½ lemon
1 teaspoon French Dijon mustard (optional)

Put the cider into a saucepan and boil rapidly until reduced to about half the quantity. Add the remaining ingredients and cook over a low heat, stirring continually, until the jelly has melted. Cool and serve cold with hot or cold tongue, ham, duck, game or turkey.

Mint Sauce

A must with anything that is to do with roast or grilled lamb.

3 tablespoons cider vinegar
2 teaspoons caster sugar
2 tablespoons very finely-chopped fresh spearmint

Heat the vinegar in a small saucepan. Add the sugar, remove from the heat and stir until the sugar is dissolved. Leave to stand for 10 minutes, then add the mint and mix well. Leave to stand for at least 1 hour before serving.

Onion Sauce

This is traditionally served with baked or braised rabbit, but try it with lamb too. I have served pink slices of young roast lamb smothered in the sauce with mint sauce and redcurrant jelly on the side, and found it a good way to produce a joint of lamb for a dinner party without having to go through all the rigmarole of carving the meat at the table for quite a large number of people. I carved the lamb before the guests sat down for dinner, poured over the sauce and covered it tightly with foil to prevent a skin forming.

> 2 large Spanish onions
> 5 oz (150 g) butter
> $\frac{1}{4}$ pint (150 ml) single cream
> Salt and white pepper

Peel and roughly chop the onions. Cook in boiling salted water until tender. Mash until fairly smooth.

Melt the butter in a small saucepan, add the onions and cook over a low heat for 5 minutes. Add the cream, season with salt and pepper and cook over a low heat, without boiling, for a further 5 minutes.

Savoury Dumplings

> 4 oz (125 g) self-raising flour
> $1\frac{1}{2}$ teaspoons mixed herbs
> Salt and freshly-ground black pepper
> 2 oz (50 g) shredded suet

Combine the flour in a bowl with the herbs and seasoning and mix well. Add the suet and mix again. Make a well in the centre and gradually stir in enough water to make a stiff dough, pulling in the flour from the sides of the bowl. Turn on to a floured board, knead lightly and using floured hands roll the mixture into eight balls.

Add the dumplings to lightly-boiling stew or soup and cook for 20 minutes.

Savoury Spiced Pears

Large chunks of pears, preserved with spices in a syrup sharpened with cider vinegar, provide one of the best possible accompaniments to cold ham, tongue or boiled beef. The pears will benefit from at least 3 months' maturing time before being opened.

1 lb (450 g) granulated sugar
1 pint (575 ml) water
Finely-grated rind of 1 orange
Finely-grated rind of 1 lemon
$\frac{1}{2}$ teaspoon ground ginger
$\frac{1}{2}$ teaspoon ground cinnamon
12 allspice berries
20 coriander seeds
1 blade mace
3 lb (1·4 kg) firm under-ripe pears (Conference)
Cloves
6 fl oz (175 ml) cider vinegar

Combine the sugar, water, orange and lemon peel in a saucepan. Bring to the boil, stirring, until the sugar has melted. Add the spices and boil for 15 minutes.

Peel and halve the pears and cut out the cores. Push a clove into each pear half. Add the pears to the syrup and cook over a low heat for 20 minutes. Remove from the heat and leave overnight in a cool place.

Remove the pears from the syrup with a slotted spoon, add the vinegar to the syrup, bring to the boil and simmer for 20 minutes. Return the pears to the syrup and cook over a low heat for 10 minutes or until they are just tender and have a transparent look. Remove them again with a slotted spoon, pack carefully into sterilised, wide-necked jars, pour over the strained syrup, filling up the jars so that the fruit is completely covered. Seal tightly and store in a cool dark place.

Rhubarb Relish

This goes well with cold ham, tongue, beef or lamb and is delicious in a plain cheese sandwich.

$\frac{1}{4}$ teaspoon ground nutmeg
$\frac{1}{4}$ teaspoon ground cloves
1 teaspoon ground cinnamon
$\frac{1}{2}$ teaspoon mixed spice
$\frac{1}{4}$ pint (150 ml) water
2 lb (900 g) granulated sugar
$\frac{1}{4}$ pint (150 ml) cider vinegar
2 lb (900 g) rhubarb
$\frac{1}{2}$ lb (225 g) stoned raisins

Tie the spices in a piece of fine muslin and combine them with the water, sugar and vinegar. Bring to the boil and simmer for 25 minutes.

Cut the rhubarb into 1-in ($2\frac{1}{2}$-cm) cubes. Remove the spices from the syrup, add the rhubarb and raisins, return to the boil and simmer for a further 40 minutes or until the mixture is really thick. Put into warm jars and seal when cold.

Rosehip and Apple Jelly

1 pint (575 ml) rosehips, freshly picked
$2\frac{1}{2}$ lb (1·1 kg) cooking apples
Juice of 1 large lemon
Sugar

Wash rosehips, cover with water, bring to the boil and simmer for about 30 minutes until soft. Mash thoroughly with a fork and strain, with the liquid from the pan, through muslin.

Roughly chop the apples, cover them with water, bring to the boil and simmer gently for about 20 minutes or until soft. Strain the liquid through a muslin bag. Measure into a clean pan and add the rosehip liquid, lemon juice and 1 lb (450 g) of sugar for every pint (575 ml) of liquid.

Bring to the boil, stirring until sugar is dissolved, and boil hard until a small amount of the jelly put into a saucer of ice-cold water will set (this will probably take about 40 minutes).

Apple and Mint Sauce

Serve with dishes which you would normally accompany with an apple sauce. The fresh mint gives the apple a piquant lift and makes the sauce into something more interesting than the usual rather bland version.

1 lb (450 g) cooking apples
1 oz (25 g) butter
1–2 oz (25–50 g) sugar
2 cloves
Salt and freshly-ground black pepper
1 tablespoon finely-chopped mint

Peel, core and rough-chop the apples. Combine the butter, apples, sugar and cloves in a saucepan, bring slowly to the boil and simmer until the apples are tender. Remove the cloves and mash to a purée. Season with salt and pepper, leave to cool and then mix in the mint.

Apple and Mint Relish

An alternative to mundane mint sauce or jelly that goes well with hot or cold lamb and with curries and spiced meat dishes.

3 crisp eating apples
2 tablespoons finely-chopped mint
1½ tablespoons caster sugar
Cider vinegar

Peel and finely chop the apples and toss them with the sugar and mint. Pour over enough cider vinegar to cover and mix lightly. Keep in a refrigerator until required.

Mint, Sage and Gooseberry Jelly

This has more body than a plain mint jelly and a better taste too, I think.

> 2 lb (900 g) green gooseberries
> 2 pints (1 litre) water
> Juice of 1 lemon
> Loaf sugar
> 6 sprigs mint
> 2 teaspoons finely-chopped sage

Top, tail and halve the gooseberries. Put in a heavy pan with the water and lemon juice, bring to the boil, lower the heat and simmer gently for 20 minutes. Put the mixture into a sieve lined with muslin and leave to drip through overnight.

Measure gooseberry liquid and combine with 1 lb (450 g) sugar for each pint (575 ml) in a large heavy pan. Bring to the boil and boil over a high heat for 5 minutes or until a small spoonful of the jelly dropped on a saucer will set.

Reserve 4 leaves of the mint and chop them very finely. Add remaining mint to the jelly as soon as it comes off the heat and leave to infuse for 10 minutes. Strain through a fine sieve.

Steep chopped mint and sage in enough boiling water to cover for 5 minutes, drain and add to the jelly. Pour into jars, cover and store in a cool dark place.

Note: Green vegetable colouring can be added to the jelly to make it more lively to look at.

Oyster Stuffing

I know it sounds ridiculous these days to use oysters as a common-or-garden stuffing, but although our native oysters are now very expensive, it is possible to buy imported oysters for a very reasonable price and these can be used equally well for stuffings. These oysters come in tins, can be bought in most delicatessens and there are 8–12 in each tin. The stuffing made with oysters is too good to overlook – serve it for a really special meal and give your guests some excitement. By the way, those unfortunates who have suffered from a bad oyster in the past should not be affected by the oysters cooked in this stuffing.

Use the stuffing for roast chicken, duck or goose.

12 oysters
2 eggs
3 oz (75 g) fresh white breadcrumbs
1 oz (25 g) shredded suet
1 tablespoon mixed finely-chopped fresh sage, parsley and thyme
Salt and freshly ground black pepper

Cut off the beards from the oysters. Beat the eggs. Cut each oyster into four and combine them with the breadcrumbs, suet and herbs. Season with salt and pepper and mix with the beaten eggs to make a firm mixture.

Stuff the chicken or duck and roast as usual.

Fried Parsley

I had always thought this garnish to be one of the more sophisticated notions of French *haute cuisine* until a friend of mine pointed out that it was written up in the kitchen notebook of an early eighteenth-century housekeeper to one of the grander Cornish houses. Serve the crisply-fried parsley with any fried fish, with fritters or, for that matter, with almost anything. It is full of iron and really delicious in its crunchiness.

Deep fat or vegetable oil for frying
12 full heads of parsley on the stalk

Heat the fat until smoking. Add the parsley stalks, not too many at a time, and cook for about a minute until the parsley curls up, turns a dark green in colour and is crisp throughout. Drain on kitchen paper and serve as soon as possible.

Forcemeat Balls

I was given this recipe by a farmer's wife in Somerset who said it was a favourite of her grandmother, who used to serve tiny balls in vegetable or clear soups and larger ones in stews that were rather on the plain side. Originally it was made with veal but since veal is so hard to find in the West Country, and expensive when you do, we both agreed that pig's or lamb's liver could be used instead.

I have found the balls freeze successfully. Frozen forcemeat can be fried from the frozen state but will, of course, require considerably longer cooking time.

2 oz (50 g) liver
1 anchovy fillet
$\frac{1}{2}$ lb (225 g) shredded beef suet
4 oz (125 g) fresh white breadcrumbs
1 teaspoon grated lemon peel
Pinch marjoram and thyme
1 egg
Freshly-ground black pepper
Flour

Mince the liver with the drained anchovy fillet. Combine the suet and the bread and pound until fairly smooth with the back of a wooden spoon. Add the liver and anchovy, the lemon peel, herbs and egg. Season with pepper and mix well until all the ingredients are incorporated, then blend in enough flour to make a stiff enough mixture to form into balls. Using a well-floured board, form the mixture into even-sized balls. Chill before using.

Fry the forcemeat balls in lard until brown on the outside

and cooked throughout (the only way to make sure of this is to have a taste).

Note: Forcemeat balls also make a good stretching ingredient if served with a roast chicken or a piece of roast meat.

Anchovy Essence and Mushroom Ketchup

Anchovy essence and mushroom ketchup were used for flavouring throughout the country up until the end of the last century. Why they went out of fashion I have no idea, for both these ingredients can make a valuable contribution to twentieth-century cooking. You can still buy anchovy essence and the mushroom ketchup if you search around a bit (a good delicatessen should stock them both) or you can use anchovies in place of the essence and make your own mushroom ketchup.

Anchovy essence was used for meat as well as for fish dishes and appeared in many classic English dishes like jugged hare, potted beef and pork pies, taking the place of salt seasoning and also giving an extra flavour that complemented the other ingredients. Mushroom ketchup is invaluable for flavouring all soups, casseroles and stews.

Relish of Runner Beans

You know how it is with runner beans: they all come at once and after a week or two the last thing you want to see again is a runner bean. You can, of course, freeze them, but as an alternative, try making a runner bean relish to serve with cold meats or poultry. I find this a great success, as the slightly crunchy texture of the beans with the pickling ingredients makes a pleasant change from an ordinary relish. In fact the beans are so good I often find guests actually treat them as a vegetable and not just a chutney.

4 lb (1·8 kg) runner beans
1 tablespoon salt
½ tablespoon turmeric
2 lb (900 g) granulated sugar
2 pints (1 litre) cider vinegar
3 tablespoons cornflour
4 tablespoons dry English mustard
Pinch celery salt

Top, tail and string beans and cut diagonally into thin slices. Cook in boiling water to which the salt and turmeric have been added until they are tender but still crisp (it is important not to overcook – test by tasting).

Combine the sugar and vinegar together, bring to the boil, stirring to dissolve the sugar, and boil for 10 minutes. Ladle off about two tablespoons of the vinegar mixture and gradually add it to the cornflour, mustard and celery salt, stirring to get a smooth paste.

Add the paste to the boiling vinegar and stir until the syrup is thick and smooth. Add the beans, mix well, transfer to warm jars and seal.

Potato Fry

Serves 4

1 lb (450 g) belly pork
1½ lb (675 g) potatoes
2 large onions
Salt and freshly-ground black pepper
Pinch sage
½ pint (275 ml) stock

Cut the pork belly into finger-thick slices. Peel and slice the potatoes. Peel and thinly slice the onions and divide into rings.

Place the pork in the bottom of a large frying pan. Cover with alternate layers of onions and potatoes finishing with a layer of potatoes and seasoning the layers with salt, pepper and a little sage. Pour over the stock. Bring to the boil, cover tightly and simmer for 1 hour or until pork belly is really tender.

Brawn

Serves 8

3 pig's trotters
2 large carrots
2 onions
Tops of 3 celery stalks
12 peppercorns
Pinch ground ginger
Pinch mace
3 cloves
2 bay leaves
1 tablespoon white wine vinegar
Salt
4 lamb's tongues
1 tablespoon tomato purée
2 hard-boiled eggs
4 oz (125 g) frozen peas

Put the pig's trotters (split in half lengthwise) into a large saucepan with the whole carrots; the onions, cut into quarters not peeled; celery tops, peppercorns, ginger, mace, cloves, bay leaves and vinegar. Amply cover with cold water and season with salt. Bring to the boil, skim off any scum that rises to the surface, cover and simmer for 1 hour.

Add the lamb's tongues and continue to simmer for a further 45–60 minutes until the tongues are tender. Remove the trotters, tongues and carrots and leave to cool. Strain the stock through muslin, add the tomato purée and boil hard for 15 minutes. Cool and leave in a refrigerator until the fat has formed a skin on the surface.

Remove the skin from the tongues and pull out any bones

or gristle from the roots. Cut the tongues into $\frac{1}{2}$-in (1-cm) dice. Cut off the meat from the trotters and chop it finely.

Thinly slice the carrots. Slice the hard-boiled eggs. Cook the peas in a little boiling water until just tender, rinse them at once in cold running water and drain them well.

Rinse a large loaf tin with cold water and line it with the slices of carrot and hard-boiled eggs. Fill the tin with layers of tongue, the meat from the trotters and the peas.

Remove the fat from the stock and heat the stock gently, if necessary, to melt the liquid to a pouring consistency. Pour the stock over the ingredients in the tin and leave in a refrigerator to set firm. Dip the tin into very hot water and turn out the brawn on to a serving dish. Surround with slices of tomato and serve, cut into thick slices, with a green salad and baked potatoes, or a potato salad.

Note: For a buffet party, a wineglass of sherry can be added to the stock to give extra flavour.

Mock Goose

There are many old-fashioned recipes which go under the name of 'Mock Goose'. This is a way of making a small leg of pork more interesting than it usually is. You don't get the crackling on the roast but this can be successfully roasted with the meat to serve on the side.

> 1 small piece leg of pork, about 3 lb (1·4 kg)
> 1 small onion
> $\frac{1}{2}$ teaspoon dried sage
> 2 oz (50 g) fine white breadcrumbs
> Salt and freshly-ground black pepper
> 3 oz (75 g) butter

Cover the leg of pork with cold water, bring to the boil and parboil for 30 minutes. Remove from the water, cool and then cut off the skin and three-quarters of the fat. (Cut the skin into ¼-in (6-mm) thick strips if you wish to crisp it by baking in the oven.)

Peel and finely chop the onion. Grind the sage to a powder in a mortar with a pestle. Add the onion, breadcrumbs and seasoning and continue to pound until the mixture is smooth. Rub the mixture all over the pork joint.

Melt the butter. Place the joint in a baking dish, pour over the butter and roast in a moderately hot oven (400° F, Reg 6). Baste frequently with the butter and roast for about 1 hour or until the pork is tender. Serve with:

Apple, onion and sage forcemeat balls
>   1 medium cooking apple
>   1 small onion, finely chopped
>   4 fresh sage leaves
>   4 oz (125 g) breadcrumbs
>   1 egg, beaten
>   Salt and freshly-ground black pepper

Peel and grate the apple. Combine all the ingredients and mix well. Using floured hands, form the forcemeat into 1½-in (3½-cm) diameter balls and fry until golden brown and crisp in very hot fat or dripping. Drain on kitchen paper and serve around the roast.

Piggly Pie

>   *Serves 4*

>   1 lb (450 g) lean pork
>   1 lb (450 g) cooking apples
>   2 onions
>   2 teaspoons sugar
>   1 teaspoon finely-grated lemon rind
>   Salt and freshly-ground black pepper
>   Pinch nutmeg

Pinch rosemary
$\frac{1}{4}$ pint (150 ml) dry cider
2 oz (50 g) butter
8 oz (225 g) puff pastry
1 small egg, beaten

Cut the pork into very thin slices. Peel, core and thinly slice the apples. Peel and slice the onions and divide into rings.

Arrange half the onion rings in a lightly-greased pie dish. Cover with half the apple slices sprinkled with a little sugar and lemon rind and then with the pork. Season with salt, pepper, pinch of nutmeg and rosemary and top with remaining apples and onions. Pour over cider and dot with butter.

Roll out the pastry to about $\frac{1}{4}$ in (6 mm) thick. Cover the pie with the pastry, damping the rim of the dish and pressing the edge of the pastry down firmly. Brush with beaten egg mixed with a little water and a pinch salt and bake in a moderately hot oven (375° F, Reg 5) for $1\frac{1}{4}$ hours.

Note: The pie crust can be lifted and about $\frac{1}{4}$ pint (150 ml) of cream poured over the ingredients before serving.

Puddletown Baked Pork Chops

This is a dish we often have at Maidenwell. It really has no particular connection with Puddletown in Dorset – I just like the name.

Serves 4

2 cloves garlic
6 juniper berries
4 pork chops
Salt and freshly-ground black pepper
1 tablespoon bacon fat
$1\frac{1}{2}$ lb (675 g) potatoes
1 large onion
4 oz (125 g) ham

1 teaspoon rosemary
¼ pint (150 ml) medium dry cider
2 tablespoons finely-chopped parsley

Peel and crush the garlic cloves; crush the juniper berries. Rub the pork chops with a mixture of the garlic and juniper berries and some pepper.

Heat the bacon fat, add the pork chops and cook over a high heat until lightly browned on each side. Peel and thinly slice the potatoes. Peel and thinly slice the onions and divide into rings. Chop the ham. Arrange half the potatoes in the bottom of a lightly-greased baking dish. Cover with half the onions and then with the pork chops. Season with salt, sprinkle over the rosemary and put the ham on top. Finish with the rest of the onions and then with the potatoes arranged in overlapping layers. Pour over the cider, cover the dish tightly with foil and cook in a slow oven (300° F, Reg 2) for about 1½–2 hours or until pork chops are absolutely tender. Spoon off any fat which has risen to the surface and sprinkle with the parsley.

Bodelver Pork

A rich and succulent roast/braise of pork belly, parsnips, potatoes and stock.

Serves 6

2½ lb (1·1 kg) pork belly
Salt and freshly-ground black pepper
Pinch thyme, sage and rosemary
1½ lb (675 g) parsnips
1½ lb (675 g) potatoes
12 small shallots
½ pint (275 ml) beef stock
2 tablespoons redcurrant jelly

Score through the skin of the pork belly with a sharp pointed knife. Rub the skin with salt, pepper and the herbs.

Peel and roughly chop the parsnips; peel and roughly chop the potatoes. Peel the shallots.

Blanch the potatoes and parsnips in boiling salted water for 5 minutes and drain well. Place the belly, skin side up, in a roasting tin, and surround with the vegetables. Combine the stock with the redcurrant jelly and heat over a low flame until the jelly has melted. Pour the stock over the meat and vegetables and roast in a moderately hot oven (400° F, Reg 6) for 2 hours, basting the vegetables every now and then.

Lift the meat and vegetables on to a serving dish and pour the gravy into a bowl. Spoon off the excess fat from the surface and serve the gravy separately in a sauceboat.

An apple sauce flavoured with a little freshly chopped mint goes well with this dish. See page 113.

Maidenwell Spiced Roast Pork

Pork is very susceptible to weather conditions and, unlike most other meat, should be eaten as fresh as possible. As I try not to do my shopping more than once a week, this can be a problem, but one that is overcome by spicing the meat. Once spiced and marinated the meat will keep happily in a refrigerator for up to five days and indeed the longer you keep it the more developed the flavours will become and the better the end result. This method of processing the meat is really just a short cut to the old salting and pickling processes that were used before the days of refrigeration.

      1 leg pork weighing about 5 lb (2·3 kg)
      4 tablespoons coarse salt
      1 tablespoon freshly-ground black pepper
      6 sage leaves
      1 sprig thyme
      1 small sprig rosemary
      4 juniper berries
      2 cloves garlic

1 teaspoon dry English mustard
½ pint (275 ml) cheap red wine
1 tablespoon flour

Using a very sharp knife, diagonally score through the skin of the pork at ½-in (1-cm) intervals. Combine the salt, pepper, herbs and spices in a mortar and grind with a pestle until the mixture is smooth. Rub the spiced mixture into the exposed flesh and the skin of the joint. Place the joint in a baking tin, pour over the wine and refrigerate for at least four days, turning the leg now and then so that it is well marinated in the wine.

Leave the leg in the tin, together with the marinade, and roast it in a moderately-hot oven (375° F, Reg 5) skin side up, for 30 minutes to the pound. If the crackling gets too brown, cover it with foil, but remove the foil for the last ten minutes of cooking time.

Transfer the leg to a serving dish and keep warm (leaving the joint to stand before carving helps to compact the meat and make carving easier). Strain off the juices from the pan and spoon off as much of the fat as possible.

Heat a dessertspoonful of the fat in a saucepan, add the flour and mix well. Gradually blend in the cooking juices, stirring continually, until the sauce becomes thick and smooth. Taste for seasoning.

Apple and Sage Sauce

A few leaves of sage added to the apple sauce gives it a good country-fresh flavour.

1½ lb (675 g) cooking apples
4 leaves sage
2 oz (50 g) butter
1 tablespoon sugar
Salt and freshly-ground black pepper

Peel and core the apples and roughly chop the flesh. Finely chop the sage. Melt half the butter in a saucepan. Add the apples, sugar and sage and cook over a low heat, stirring every now and then to prevent sticking, until the apples are soft. Purée with a potato masher or through a food mill and return to a clean pan. Beat in the remaining butter and season with salt and pepper. Heat through and serve hot with the pork.

Fried Petitoes (Pig's Trotters)

Serves 4

4 pig's trotters
1 teaspoon salt
2 teaspoons white wine or cider vinegar
1 carrot
1 onion
1½ pints (875 ml) stock
Bouquet garni
1 egg, beaten
2 oz (50 g) browned breadcrumbs
Salt and freshly-ground black pepper
Lard or dripping for frying
1 shallot
1 tablespoon white wine vinegar
2 oz (50 g) butter
1 teaspoon made English or Dijon mustard

Clean the trotters, cover them with cold water to which a teaspoon of salt has been added and leave to stand for 2 hours. Drain well and put the trotters in a saucepan. Add the 2 teaspoons of vinegar, carrot peeled and roughly chopped, onion peeled and chopped, and pour over enough stock to cover. Add the bouquet garni, bring to the boil, cover and simmer for about 2½ hours until tender. Drain well and leave until cool enough to handle.

Cut each trotter in half, lengthwise, and coat in egg and breadcrumbs. Season with salt and pepper. Fry the trotters until crisp and golden brown in hot lard or dripping and drain on kitchen paper.

Peel and finely chop the shallot. Combine the shallot and 1 tablespoon white wine vinegar in a saucepan and boil until shallot is soft and vinegar absorbed. Add the butter, cut into small pieces and cook, stirring continually, over a low heat until the butter has melted. Add the mustard and mix well.

Spoon a little sauce over each of the trotters before serving.

Devonshire Lamb Stew

This early summer stew is one of the best ways of cooking and stretching the good flavour of plump lamb chops.

Serves 4

4 plump lamb chops
1 lb (450 g) new potatoes
2 oz (50 g) firm button mushrooms
8 baby carrots
8 small shallots
1 oz (25 g) butter
¼ pint (150 ml) cider
¼ pint (150 ml) chicken stock
Salt and freshly-ground black pepper
Bouquet garni made of a sprig thyme, parsley and lovage
4 oz (125 g) peas
2½ fl oz (75 ml) double cream
2 tablespoons finely-chopped parsley

Trim off excess fat from the chops. Scrape the new potatoes, cutting any large ones into walnut-sized pieces. Thinly slice the mushrooms. Clean the carrots. Peel the shallots, leaving them whole.

Melt the butter in a heavy frying pan. Add the chops and fry over a medium heat until lightly browned. Remove to a flameproof casserole with a slotted spoon. Add the potatoes, shallots and carrots to the juices in the pan, cook over a low heat for about 3 minutes until golden and transfer to the casserole.

Mix in the cider and stock to the juices in the pan. Bring to the boil and pour the liquid over the chops and vegetables. Season with salt and pepper, add the bouquet garni, cover and simmer for 45 minutes. Mix in the peas and continue to cook for a further 15 minutes. Stir in the cream and parsley and heat through without boiling.

Serve the stew with a green vegetable.

Boiled Lamb with Parsley Dumplings

This rich and nourishing dish is easily enough to serve eight. Any left over can be used in the same way as roast meat.

Serves 8

4 carrots
2 large onions
1½ oz (40 g) butter
Salt and freshly-ground black pepper
1 small leg lamb
Pinch sage, rosemary and thyme
2 bay leaves
1 pint (575 ml) rich stock
6 oz (175 g) fresh white breadcrumbs
3 oz (75 g) shredded suet
3 tablespoons finely-chopped parsley
Grated rind of ½ lemon
1 large egg, lightly beaten
2 teaspoons cornflour

Peel and thickly slice the carrots. Peel and roughly chop the onions. Melt the butter in a large fireproof casserole or heavy saucepan. Add the carrots and onions and cook over a low heat until the onions are soft and transparent. Season the leg of lamb and place it on top of the vegetables, sprinkle over the sage, rosemary, thyme and bay leaves and pour over the stock. Bring to the boil, cover tightly and simmer for 20 minutes to the pound.

Make the dumplings while the lamb is cooking. Mix the breadcrumbs with the suet and parsley. Add the lemon rind, season with salt and pepper and mix in the beaten egg, beating the mixture well.

Add the dumpling mixture to the boiled leg, dropping it from a dessertspoon into the stock surrounding the joint, and boil for a further 20 minutes.

Remove the bay leaves. Lift out the leg and put it in a deep serving dish surrounded by the vegetables and dumplings lifted out with a slotted spoon.

Add a spoonful of the cooking liquid to the cornflour and mix to a smooth paste. Add the paste to the stock, bring to the boil and stir until nicely thickened. Check seasoning and strain the gravy into a sauceboat.

Serve with a mint or caper sauce.

Parsley Dumplings

Add these savoury and aromatic dumplings to any stew or country soup to stretch more expensive ingredients and to provide a satisfying addition to a main course dish.

Serves 4–6

6 oz (175 g) fresh white breadcrumbs
3 oz (75 g) shredded suet
3 tablespoons very finely-chopped parsley
Pinch finely-chopped thyme and sage
Grated rind of $\frac{1}{2}$ lemon
Salt and freshly-ground black pepper
1 large egg, beaten

Combine breadcrumbs, shredded suet, parsley, thyme and sage and lemon rind in a bowl. Season with salt and pepper, add the beaten egg and beat with a wooden spoon until well mixed.

Slide dessertspoonfuls of the dumpling mixture into boiling soup or stew and cook for 20 minutes before serving.

Lamb Chops Marinated in Honey and Cider

Serves 4

4 large or 8 small lamb chops
2 tablespoons vinegar
1 tablespoon olive oil
$\frac{1}{2}$ tablespoon runny honey
$\frac{1}{2}$ teaspoon mixed marjoram and rosemary
4 tablespoons dry cider
Freshly-ground black pepper

Trim the chops of excess fat. Combine all the ingredients for the marinade, pour over the chops and leave to stand in a refrigerator overnight.

Place the chops on a rack and grill them under a high heat, basting every now and then with the marinade until the chops are well browned on the outside but slightly pink in the centre.

Serve the chops with the juices from the pan poured over them and with mashed potatoes and a watercress salad.

Wiltshire Shoulder of Herbed Lamb

This is an eighteenth-century West Country way of cooking lamb that not only gives a delicious herby flavour that melts into the joint but also provides a rich basting juice to keep the joint moist and, in the end, make a most delicious gravy.

Serves 6

1 shoulder of English lamb
4 tablespoons flour

2 teaspoons mixed rubbed rosemary, sage and thyme
Coarse cooking salt and freshly-ground black pepper
$\frac{1}{2}$ pint (275 ml) boiling water
2 tablespoons strong stock or rich meat drippng
1 tablespoon plum or damson jam or redcurrant jelly

Score the skin of the lamb shoulder. Combine the flour, herbs and plenty of coarse salt and pepper and rub the mixture into the scored skin and the cut side of the joint. Place the meat in a baking dish.

Combine the boiling water with the stock or meat drippings and the jelly or jam, mix well and pour over the meat. Cook in a slow oven (300° F, Reg 2) for $2\frac{1}{4}$ hours, basting frequently with the juices in the pan. Remove the joint on to a serving plate and keep warm.

Wring out a piece of muslin in cold water and strain the juices from the pan through this cloth so that all the fat is collected and the gravy is clear.

Serve the lamb whenever possible with boiled new potatoes, young peas and young runner beans.

Mustard Grilled Kidneys

Sheep's and more recently lambs' kidneys have always been popular in the West Country where folk were never ones to turn their noses up at a bit of offal. Good use was made of every bit of the sheep including delicious pies and other dishes made from lambs' tails (see page 89).

Originally this would have been a breakfast dish. Now it makes a good light lunch or supper dish.

Serves 4

8 lambs' kidneys
2 teaspoons made English mustard
Freshly-ground black pepper
3 oz (75 g) melted butter
Salt

Split the kidneys three-quarters of the way through, leaving a flap at the core side. Strip off any fat and the skin and open the kidneys out flat. Lightly score on the uncut side and rub mustard on both sides. Season with plenty of pepper. Run a skewer through the kidneys to prevent them from curling up. Brush with melted butter and grill under a hot flame for 3 minutes. Turn, baste with the juices and grill for a further 3 minutes.

Sprinkle with a little salt before serving.

Note: The kidneys are salted after rather than before cooking to prevent too much of the juice oozing out. Salt on cut meat draws the juice to the surface.

Boiled Brisket with Herbs

Having served this hot for a Sunday lunch, I then press the beef to serve cold for later meals.

Serves 6

3–4 lb (1·4–1·8 kg) boned and rolled brisket
Flour
Salt and freshly-ground black pepper
2 rashers streaky bacon
3 large onions
4 carrots
2 sticks celery
1 oz (25 g) dripping or lard
½ pint (275 ml) pale ale
3 teaspoons dark brown sugar
½ teaspoon allspice
4 sprigs parsley
Sprig summer savory

Roll the meat in flour seasoned with salt and pepper until it is well coated. Cut the rind off the bacon and chop the rashers. Peel and roughly chop the onions and carrots. Discard the leaves and roughly chop the celery sticks.

Melt the dripping in a deep frying pan, add the bacon, carrots, onions and celery and cook over a low heat until the vegetables are softened and the onion is a pale golden colour. Transfer the vegetables with a slotted spoon to a flameproof casserole and place the meat on top.

Pour the light ale into the juice the vegetables were cooked in and mix in the sugar. Season with a little salt and pepper and the allspice and stir over a medium high heat for 1 minute. Pour the liquid over the meat, top the meat with the herbs, cover tightly and cook over a low heat for 2½ hours until the meat is tender.

Discard the herbs, remove the meat on to a heated serving dish and surround with the vegetables. Serve the gravy separately.

Note: To press the remains of the meat for serving cold put into a cake tin just large enough to take the meat, preferably with a removable base, pour over any remains of gravy with the fat removed and press with a heavy weight on a plate. Leave in a refrigerator for at least 8 hours before removing the tin and serving cold with salad.

Under Roast

A good combination of shin beef and kidney with a crisp topping of potatoes.

Serves 4–6

2 lb (900 g) shin beef
8 oz (225 g) kidney
1 lb (450 g) onions
2 large carrots
8 oz (225 g) swede
1½ lb (675 g) potatoes

Flour
Salt and freshly-ground black pepper
2 tablespoons dripping
1¼ pints (725 ml) stock

Remove any tough sinews from the meat and cut it into small dice. Trim the hard centre core from the kidney and cut into small pieces. Peel and roughly chop the onions. Peel and dice the carrots and swede. Peel the potatoes and cut into pieces about the size of a small egg.

Combine some flour with a generous seasoning of salt and pepper. Roll the meat in seasoned flour until well coated. Melt the dripping in a flameproof casserole, add the meat and brown over a high heat on all sides. Remove the meat with a slotted spoon. Add the onions, carrots and swede to the juices in the casserole and cook over a lowish heat until the onions are soft and transparent. Add the meat, pour over the stock, bring to the boil, cover and simmer for 30 minutes.

Place the potatoes on top of the stew so that they are half in and half out of the stock. Do not replace the cover of the casserole. Cook in a moderate oven (325° F, Reg 3) for 2 hours until the meat is cooked and the tops of the potatoes are crisp and golden brown.

China Chilo

In researching into old West Country cookery books I found many references to this curiously-named dish of minced meat served in a ring of boiled rice. This version came from a beautifully handwritten, leather-bound book dating from the early nineteenth century, lent to me by Vee. It came from a house called Wood where her husband Geoff had been the head gardener of one of the finest Devon gardens.

In the book the recipe called for five cucumbers, and no serving quantities were given, so I tried it out with the following ingredients and found it was a good dish with an interesting texture.

Serves 6

1½ lb (675 g) chuck steak
3 sprigs thyme
1 cucumber
1 lettuce
4 shallots or 2 onions
4 oz (125 g) butter
¼ pint (150 ml) strong stock or gravy
Salt and freshly-ground pepper
12 oz (350 g) long grained rice

Remove any skin or gristle from the meat but leave on any fat. Mince the meat finely. Shred the thyme leaves off the stalks. Peel and cut the cucumber into small dice. Clean and finely shred the lettuce leaves. Peel and finely chop the shallots.

Melt the butter, add the onion and cook over a low heat until soft and transparent. Raise the heat, add meat and brown over a fast flame, stirring every now and then until the meat is a good dark colour. Add cucumber, lettuce and thyme and cook for 2 minutes. Add gravy or stock, mix well, season with salt and pepper and simmer for 1 hour or until very tender.

Put the rice into a saucepan, pour over enough cold water to come 1 in (2½ cm) over the top of the rice and add ½ teaspoon salt. Bring to the boil, stirring every now and then, cover tightly and boil until water has all been absorbed by the rice and the rice is tender and fluffy – take care not to boil so dry that the rice at the bottom burns.

Pile the rice in a ring around a serving dish and spoon the 'chilo' into the centre.

5

Country Game Bag

My deep freeze is healthily filled with pheasants, the odd wild duck, woodcock and snipe. Rabbits also play a part in our seasonal diet, as does the occasional hare.

THE SECRET of good game cooking lies in the hanging of the birds and in finding the right recipe to suit their age and condition. All game needs to be hung in order to tenderise the flesh and develop that all-important game flavour, and the time you allow for this process will depend both on the weather conditions at the time and on individual taste. I go by a conservative rule of hanging all birds for eight days in cold weather, and for five in more warm or muggy temperatures.

Birds that are no longer young should never be roasted. The result will always be disappointing with the flesh dry and tough, and no amount of basting or slow careful cooking is going to change this. If their age is in any doubt, stick to long, slow cooking methods such as casseroling or use the birds to make a well-flavoured and exciting pâté.

Make sure that all frozen game is thoroughly defrosted before being cooked and if possible do this overnight in a refrigerator.

RABBITS

The West Country is alive with rabbits that are fortunately, at the time I am writing this, quite free from that horrible disease, myxomatosis. I am always torn between loving to watch them hopping around the fields and lanes and cursing them for the damage they do to the land and to the young plants in my garden, but my softheartedness doesn't prevent me accepting rabbits for the pot with pleasure.

Most rabbits you buy from the supermarkets these days are imported and reared especially for eating. Our wild ones are not quite so fat and meaty, but they are full of flavour and make good eating. For some recipes, this flavour can be just a little too strong and you may find it advisable to soak the joints in cold water before cooking them.

Unlike other game, rabbits should not be hung before being skinned and paunched, and in fact, the sooner you deal with them, the better.

Rabbit Pâté

Use as a first course pâté or as a sandwich spread.

> 1 rabbit
> 12 oz (350 g) fat bacon
> 1 small onion
> Pinch marjoram and thyme
> 2 teaspoons finely-chopped parsley
> Pinch mace and ground nutmeg
> Salt and freshly-ground black pepper
> 1 tablespoon brandy
> 2 oz (50 g) butter

Cut the meat off the rabbit carcass and mince it twice with the bacon and onion, through the fine blades of a mincing machine. Add the herbs, season with salt, pepper and a pinch of mace and nutmeg and stir in the brandy. Mix really well and pack into an earthenware pot or terrine. Cover tightly with two layers of foil and bake in a moderate oven (325° F, Reg 3) for 2 hours or until the pâté is coming away from the sides of the dish. Cover the terrine with a plate, weight down and leave to set.

Bring the butter to boiling point and strain it over the pâté through a layer of muslin.

Dorset Rabbit

Serves 4

> 1 young, tender rabbit
> Flour
> Salt and freshly-ground black pepper
> 6 thin rashers streaky bacon
> 4 onions
> 6 leaves sage
> 1 small egg, beaten
> 1 tablespoon milk

8 oz (225 g) fresh white breadcrumbs
1 teaspoon made English mustard
Grated peel of 1 lemon
¼ pint (150 ml) stock

Soak the prepared rabbit in cold salted water for 4 hours. Drain, wipe dry and cut into joints. Roll the joints in seasoned flour until well coated. Wrap each joint with a rasher of bacon with the rind removed. Peel and finely chop the onions. Finely chop the sage. Beat the egg with the milk. Combine the breadcrumbs, mustard, finely-chopped sage leaves, lemon peel and onion. Add the egg and milk mixture and mix well to form a thick paste. Spread the paste over the bacon-wrapped rabbit joints and arrange them in a casserole.

Pour over the stock and bake without a cover in a moderate oven (325° F, Reg 3) for about 1¼ hours or until the rabbit is tender and the coating a crisp brown. Cover the casserole with a piece of dampened greaseproof paper if the rabbit begins to brown too much during the cooking time. Serve the rabbit joints on a dish with the juices from the casserole poured over.

Rabbit Brawn

Serves 6

1 large or 2 small rabbits
2 pig's trotters
2 carrots
2 onions
2 sage leaves
2 bay leaves
Pinch mace
2 cloves
12 peppercorns
Salt
2 hard-boiled eggs

Joint the rabbit, cover it in cold water and leave to soak in salted water for 2 hours. Split the trotters lengthwise down the middle. Wash and roughly chop the carrots. Quarter the onions leaving the skins on.

Put the trotters in a heavy pan with the carrots, onions, sage and bay leaves, a pinch of mace, the cloves and the peppercorns. Season with a little salt, cover with cold water, bring slowly to the boil and skim off any scum that rises to the surface. Cover tightly and simmer for 2 hours.

Add the rabbit to the trotters and pour in a little more water if necessary (all the ingredients should be covered). Bring back to the boil and continue to simmer for a further $1\frac{1}{2}$ hours or until the rabbit meat is falling from the bones.

Remove the rabbit joints and trotters and strain the stock into a clean pan. Boil the stock over a high heat for 15 minutes and strain through a muslin-lined sieve. Leave to cool and then chill in a refrigerator until the fat forms a skin over the surface.

Cut the meat from the bones, removing any excess fatty skin from the trotters. Cut the meat into small dice. Slice the hard-boiled eggs. Remove the fat from the surface of the stock and reheat the stock gently until it is liquid but not hot.

Rinse out a bowl with cold water and arrange the slices of egg around it. Fill the bowl with the rabbit and trotter meat and pour over the liquid stock. Chill in a refrigerator until set firm. Dip the bowl into very hot water and turn out the brawn on to a serving dish.

Serve cut into wedge slices with salad and fresh, crusty bread and butter.

PIGEONS

As any farmer knows, pigeons are pretty to look at but sheer murder during the spring and early summer. If it isn't the spring cabbage they are nibbling at, it's the barley or corn, the young peas or the first show of beans. We have a pair of white pigeons nesting in one of our barns and we cannot bear to shoot them, but stalwart work is done by others to protect the rest of the farm from the ravages of these charming birds.

Victor, the milkman, provides me with some pigeons and various members of the local police force bang off against the rest in their spare time. In the spring pigeon is often on my menus, especially since I learnt a simple trick that saves all the bother of plucking them. If you have plenty of pigeons to deal with, forget about plucking them, merely cut along the breast bone with a razor-sharp knife and peel off the skin and feathers from each side. Carefully slice out the breast, which is by far the best part of a pigeon, and use this meat only – it may seem wasteful but there are times when even that makes sense.

Pigeons with Peas, Stuffed and Stewed

There are still plenty of wild pigeons around and, provided someone else shoots them, I am delighted to have them in the kitchen (see notes for preparing game on page 137).

Serves 4

4 slices white bread
1 tablespoon shredded suet
1 teaspoon finely-chopped marjoram, thyme, sage and parsley
1 teaspoon finely-grated lemon peel
Pinch ground cloves, mace and nutmeg
Salt and freshly-ground black pepper
4 young pigeons, plucked and drawn (they must be young for this dish)
2 rashers streaky bacon
4 oz (125 g) mushrooms
2 oz (50 g) butter
Flour
1 pint (575 ml) rich stock
1 teaspoon lemon juice

$\frac{1}{2}$ teaspoon Harvey's sauce or mushroom ketchup (from
good delicatessen shops)
1 lb (450 g) peas

Grate the bread, after removing the crusts, through the coarse side of a grater. Combine the bread, suet, herbs, spices and lemon peel, season with a little salt and pepper and moisten with just enough boiling water to make a workable mixture. Stuff the cavities of the pigeons with this mixture.

Remove the rinds from the bacon and finely chop the rashers. Finely chop the mushrooms. Melt the butter in a saucepan, add the bacon and mushrooms and cook over a low heat for 10 minutes, stirring to prevent sticking. Strain off the juices from the pan.

Roll the pigeons in seasoned flour until well coated all over. Heat the juices from the bacon and mushrooms in a frying pan, add the pigeons and cook over a high heat, turning the birds continually until they are golden brown on all sides. Lift out the birds with a slotted spoon and place them in a casserole with the mushrooms and bacon.

Add 1$\frac{1}{2}$ tablespoons of flour to the juices in the frying pan and stir over a medium-high heat until the flour is browned. Gradually add the stock, stirring continually until the sauce comes to the boil and is thick and smooth. Add the lemon juice and a little Harvey's sauce or mushroom ketchup.

Pour the stock over the pigeons, cover very tightly and cook in a moderate oven (350° F, Reg 4) for 1$\frac{1}{2}$ hours or until the birds are tender – this will depend on age.

Cook the peas in a little boiling salted water to which a pinch of sugar has been added. Strain well and add to the pigeons for the last 10 minutes of cooking time. Lift out the pigeons and surround with the bacon, mushrooms, peas and gravy.

PHEASANT

Most farmers' wives are on the receiving end of the game bag some time during the year, and since it is a source of free food one is usually grateful to be given the odd brace of pheasant, partridge, pigeons, woodcock or whatever happens to be around.

In the days when my husband used to shoot three or four times a week throughout the winter I became spoilt. The woodcock, occasional hare, the pigeons and above all the wild duck I loved, but the majority of the game was always pheasant, a highly overrated, usually tough and rather tasteless bird. I grew to hate the sight of them, and dreaded the endless dinner parties at other country houses where, for the same reasons of economy, pheasant featured on every menu, inevitably served up in a cream sauce with apples and Calvados, or cooked in red wine with shallots.

Now I probably only get about a dozen pheasants a year, and so treat them with less disdain, especially since I worked out a first-rate way of stretching one pheasant to make two delicious dishes for a considerable number of people. Knowing what to do with one lone pheasant is often a problem – too much for two and not enough meat for four – but by making half into a rich, very superior game pâté and the other half into an aromatic, well-flavoured soup you have the perfect solution. Both the pâté and the soup freeze well and do not taste out of place when the season is over.

Pheasant (or Partridge) Pâté

I worked out this pâté recipe for a series of demonstrations I was doing at the 1976 Game Fair. It took eight pheasants (two pâtés to a pheasant) to get it right and I cooked pâtés solidly for two days.

A partridge can be substituted for the half pheasant or you can use the same recipe to make an equally good hare, pigeon or wild duck pâté.

If you don't have fresh herbs use one of those bouquets garnis in little muslin bags.

Serves 8–10

½ pheasant
4 oz (125 g) lean ham
1 lb (450 g) fat belly pork
8 oz (225 g) pig's liver
3 thick rashers fat bacon
2 cloves garlic
6 juniper berries
Salt and freshly-ground black pepper
Pinch mace, ginger and nutmeg
3 tablespoons brandy
2 sprigs parsley
1 sprig marjoram
1 sprig thyme (lemon thyme is best)
2 bay leaves

Take the skin off the bird and reserve it to use for the soup. Cut the breast of the pheasant and the ham into very small cubes. Remove any tough ligaments or fibres from the rest of the meat. Take off the skin of the pork belly and mince the pork, liver, pheasant meat, 2 rashers of bacon with the rinds removed, garlic and juniper berries twice through the fine blades of a mincing machine.

Put the minced mixture in a bowl, season it with plenty of salt and pepper and add the spices. Beat with a wooden spoon until all the ingredients are really well amalgamated and the mixture is smooth. Add the cubed pheasant, ham and brandy and mix well.

Generously grease a 2-pint (1-litre) terrine dish with butter, pack in the pâté mixture and press it down firmly with the back of a wooden spoon. Top with the fresh herbs or bouquet garni and wrap it in tinfoil to seal it completely. Place the pâté in a baking dish, pour in enough water to come half way up the sides of the terrine and bake in a slow oven (300° F, Reg 2) for 1¾ hours. Remove the terrine from the baking tin, unwrap, remove the herbs and cover with a plate on top of which you have put a heavy weight. Leave to set overnight in a refrigerator.

Next day remove the weight, run a knife dipped in boiling water around the sides of the pâté and dip the dish itself into boiling water for 30 seconds. Turn out on to a dish and trim up any untidy edges. Cut into fairly thin slices to serve.

Note: Turning out pâtés always tends to be a rather tricky business and you may prefer to serve it in its dish. Any mucky bits around the edge can be wiped off with a cloth dipped in boiling water.

Casserole of Pheasant with Cider and Apples

Serves 4

1 pheasant
3 tablespoons flour
Salt and freshly-ground black pepper
3 stalks celery
1 medium onion
1 large cooking apple
1 oz (25 g) butter
2 tablespoons olive or vegetable oil
1 tablespoon brandy
¼ pint (150 ml) good chicken stock
½ pint (275 ml) dry cider
Bouquet garni
2 crisp eating apples
1½ oz (40 g) melted butter
¼ pint (150 ml) double cream

Dust the pheasant all over with two tablespoons of flour seasoned with salt and pepper. Slice the celery stalks. Peel and chop the onion. Peel, core and thickly slice the cooking apple. Heat the butter and oil in a large, heavy frying pan.

Add the pheasant and brown it on all sides over a high heat. Heat the brandy in a spoon, set it alight and pour it over the pheasant.

Remove the pheasant to a large casserole when the flames die down and add the onions to the juices in the pan. Cook the onions over a low heat until soft and transparent and add the celery, blend in the remaining flour and add the stock and cider, stirring over a medium heat until the sauce is thick and smooth.

Surround the pheasant with the sliced apple, pour over the sauce and the vegetables from the frying pan, add the bouquet garni, cover tightly and cook in a moderate oven (350° F, Reg 4) for 1¼ hours until the pheasant is tender.

Peel, core and thinly slice the eating apples and fry the slices in the melted butter, over a low heat, until they are golden and transparent.

Transfer the pheasant to a warm serving dish. Sieve or purée the vegetables and sauce (thin it if necessary with a little extra stock). Add the cream and heat through without boiling.

Serve the pheasant garnished with the apple slices and with the sauce on the side.

Partridge with Wine and Mushrooms

Use old partridges for this dish.

> 2 old partridges
> 2 oz (50 g) melted butter
> 4 slices streaky bacon
> 1 onion
> 2 sticks celery
> 1 carrot
> 12 oz (350 g) firm button mushrooms
> Bouquet garni
> Salt and finely-ground black pepper
> 2 oz (50 g) butter

1½ tablespoons flour
1 tablespoon redcurrant jelly
¼ pint (150 ml) full-bodied red wine
4 slices white bread with the crusts removed
Lard for frying
1 tablespoon finely-chopped parsley

Place the drawn and cleaned partridges in a roasting tin and brush them inside and outside with melted butter. Cover them with the bacon rashers and roast them in a hot oven (400° F, Reg 6) for 30 minutes, basting the birds frequently with the juices in the pan. Reserve the juices in the pan and leave the birds until cool enough to handle.

Wash but do not peel the onion and cut it into quarters. Roughly chop the celery. Clean and roughly chop the carrot. Remove the stalks from the mushrooms.

Using a small sharp knife, cut the flesh from the partridges and remove the skin if it is at all tough. Cut the flesh into neat strips roughly 1 in (2½ cm) wide by 2 in (5 cm) long.

Place the partridge carcasses in a large pan with the onion, celery and carrot and bouquet garni. Season with salt and pepper, pour over enough cold water to cover, bring to the boil, cover and simmer for 1½ hours. Strain the stock through a very fine sieve or muslin.

Melt the remaining 2 oz (50 g) of butter in a medium-sized saucepan, add the mushroom caps and cook over a medium-high heat, shaking the pan for 3 minutes. Remove the mushrooms with a slotted spoon. Add the juices from the roasting pan and mix in the flour. Mix in the redcurrant jelly and gradually blend in the red wine and enough stock to make a rich, fairly thick and smooth sauce. Add the partridge and mushrooms and simmer for 5 minutes.

Cut the bread into triangles and fry them in lard until they are crisp and brown. Drain well on kitchen paper.

Garnish the dish with triangles of fried bread and sprinkle over the chopped parsley before serving.

Woodcock and Snipe

Leave the heads on when plucking the birds and do not draw them as the entrails help to add richness and flavour to the cooked birds. Stick the beaks of the birds through their upper legs, pinning the legs to their bodies.

Brush the birds all over with melted butter and place each one on a thick slice of white bread in a roasting tin.

Cover birds completely with slices of fat streaky bacon and put them in a moderate oven (375° F, Reg 5) for 10 minutes. Remove the bacon to the side of the tin, baste the birds with any juices in the pan and continue to cook for a further 5 minutes to brown the skin.

Serve the birds on the toast and accompany them with quarters of lemon and a thin gravy.

6

Goose, Chicken and Duck

Upside, downside, stuffed or jointed, the West Country has good recipes for any poultry with ways to keep it juicy, stretch and turn it from something mundane to a dish of delicacy that is out of the ordinary.

Spiced Oranges

Delicious with pork, duck or goose.

3 Jaffa oranges
$\frac{1}{2}$ in (1 cm) stick cinnamon
4 cloves
2 blades mace
1$\frac{1}{2}$ lb (675 g) loaf sugar
$\frac{1}{2}$ pint (275 ml) cider vinegar

Cut oranges, with peel, into $\frac{1}{4}$-in (6-mm) thick slices. Put into a heavy pan and cover with cold water. Bring to the boil and simmer for 30–40 minutes until orange peel is tender. Drain slices and reserve the liquid. Tie the spices in a piece of muslin. Combine the sugar vinegar, and spices in a pan and bring slowly to the boil, stirring until the sugar is dissolved. Add orange slices and enough of the liquid in which they were cooked to cover and simmer slowly for 40 minutes. Leave to stand overnight.

Remove the spices, lift out the orange slices with a slotted spoon and pack them in warm jars. Bring the syrup to the boil and boil hard until thickened; pour over the orange slices and cover tightly.

Leave for 6–8 weeks before using.

Superior Bread Sauce

The sauce is very good to serve with roast pork but I have even sent it to the table with roast lamb and found the flavours went well together – it has a chameleon quality.

2 large onions
1$\frac{1}{2}$ oz (40 g) butter
$\frac{3}{4}$ pint (425 ml) good strong stock (this can be made
    from water added to meat drippings
1 teaspoon dried sage
2 oz (50 g) freshly-grated white breadcrumbs
Salt and freshly-ground black pepper

Peel and very finely chop the onions. Melt the butter, add the onions and cook over a low heat until soft. Raise the heat and continue to cook until they turn golden brown. Add the stock and sage, bring to the boil and simmer for 3 minutes. Add the breadcrumbs, season with salt and pepper, mix well and continue to simmer for a further 10 minutes.

Apple and Raisin Sauce

A good sauce to serve with goose or duck; the raisins enrich the sauce and add flavour to it. It also has more lemon than usual in it.

Serves 6

1 lb (450 g) cooking apples
Grated rind of ½ lemon
Juice of 1 lemon
½ oz (15 g) butter
1 oz (25 g) raisins
Sugar
Salt and freshly-ground black pepper

Peel, core and chop the apple. Combine the apples with the lemon rind and lemon juice in a saucepan, bring to the boil and cook over a low heat until tender. Remove from the heat and mash the apples until smooth with the butter, using a potato ricer or a wire whisk.

Add the raisins to the apple sauce and return to a low heat. Cook, stirring to prevent sticking, until the raisins are soft. Add enough sugar to take the edge off the apples, beating until it has dissolved, and season with salt and pepper.

Note: A pinch of sage can be added to this sauce, especially if it is to be served with roast goose.

ROAST GOOSE

Roast goose should be served with an apple sauce and be stuffed with an aromatic sage and onion stuffing. The amount of servings obviously varies according to the size of the goose and the skill of the carver. A jar of reasonably inexpensive duck pâté added to the stuffing makes a delicious dish in its own right, removed from the cavity and cut into thin slices. With the cold goose, I have a green salad and a salad of orange slices combined with cold broad beans.

Roast Goose with Stuffing

The goose liver
1 oz (25 g) melted butter
6 oz (175 g) breadcrumbs
4 oz (125 g) finely-chopped raw onions
Salt and freshly-ground black pepper
1 oz (25 g) finely-chopped fresh sage
1 goose
Flour

Very finely chop the goose liver. Melt the butter in a frying pan, add the liver and cook over a medium-high heat for a few minutes until lightly browned. Add the liver and juices from the pan to the breadcrumbs and onion, season with salt and pepper and mix in the chopped sage. Stuff the goose with this mixture. Rub the bird all over with seasoned flour and spread with goose fat if there is enough (there may not be with a young bird) or with softened butter.

Roast the bird for 30 minutes in a moderately hot oven (400° F, Reg 6). Then prick the bird all over, just through the skin and not right through to the flesh, if it is on the fat side – this is to release the excess fat from under the skin. Baste well and return to a moderate oven (350° F, Reg 4) and cook for 1–1½ hours depending on the size. With a fat goose prick the skin again after the first hour's cooking time.

Cover the legs, wings and breast with foil or greaseproof paper if the skin begins to brown too much.

Test to see if the bird is cooked by pulling the legs away from the body. If it is done the legs will flex and the flesh around the end of the leg joints will have shrunk.

Leave the bird to stand for 5 minutes before carving and make a rich gravy from the juices in the pan from which most of the fat has been poured off.

Chicken and Apple Casserole

Serves 4

4 chicken joints or 1 chicken jointed
Flour
Salt and pepper
3 apples
2 large onions
$3\frac{1}{2}$ oz (100 g) butter
$\frac{1}{2}$ pint (275 ml) medium dry cider
$\frac{1}{4}$ pint (150 ml) stock
2 sprigs parsley
Small sprig thyme
$\frac{1}{4}$ pint (150 ml) double cream

Coat the chicken joints in seasoned flour. Peel, core and roughly chop two of the apples. Peel and roughly chop the onions. Melt $2\frac{1}{2}$ oz (65 g) of butter in a heavy pan. Add the chicken joints and cook until golden brown on all sides. Lift out with a slotted spoon and place in a heatproof casserole. Add the onions and apples to the juices in the pan and cook over a low heat, without browning, until the onions are soft and transparent. Remove with a slotted spoon and add to the chicken.

Stir in 1 oz (25 g) of flour and blend in the cider and stock, stirring continually over a high heat until the liquid comes to the boil. Pour the stock from the pan over the chicken, place the herbs on top and cover tightly. Bake in a moderate oven (350° F, Reg 4) for 20–30 minutes until the chicken is tender (the time will depend on the size of the joints and the length of time it took to brown them).

Discard the herbs. Remove the chicken, onions and apples to a serving dish and keep warm. Bring the sauce to the boil and boil hard for 5 minutes to reduce it by about one-third; remove from the heat and blend in the cream.

Peel, core and slice the remaining apple and cook in the remaining butter until the slices are brown. Pour the sauce over the chicken and garnish with the fried apple slices.

West Country Chicken and Steak

An extremely rich but nevertheless exceptionally delicious dish. The contrast of textures between the meat and the poultry is a good one and this is an excellent dish to serve at a really special dinner party.

Serves 8

4 oz (125 g) butter
Pinch rosemary
Salt and freshly-ground black pepper
1 lemon
1 small roasting chicken
3 lb (1·4 kg) potatoes
$\frac{1}{2}$ pint (275 ml) double cream
Pinch ground nutmeg
1 teaspoon made English mustard
1 tablespoon finely-chopped parsley
$\frac{1}{2}$ tablespoon finely-chopped chives
$1\frac{1}{2}$ lb (675 g) rump steak
1 tablespoon olive oil

Combine half of the butter with the rosemary, season with salt and pepper and mix well. Halve the lemon. Place the halves in the cavity of the chicken and rub the bird all over with the seasoned butter. Roast in a moderately hot oven (400° F, Reg 6) for 20 minutes, then lower the heat to moderate (350° F, Reg 4) and continue to cook for a further hour or until the bird is tender. Baste frequently with the juices in the pan during the cooking time. Leave the chicken to cool.

Remove the flesh from the chicken, discard the skin and cut the flesh into small dice.

Peel the potatoes and boil until soft, drain and mash until smooth with 2 tablespoons of the double cream and 1 oz (25 g) of butter. Season with salt, pepper and a pinch of nutmeg and keep warm.

Combine the chicken with the double cream in a saucepan. Add the mustard, parsley and chives, season with a little salt and pepper and cook over a low heat until hot through. Keep warm.

Cut the rump into eight small steaks and beat flat with a meat mallet or rolling pin. Season with a little pepper (not salt as this draws out the juices). Heat 1 oz (25 g) of butter in a heavy pan with the olive oil, add the steaks and cook over a very high heat until the steaks are done (2 minutes a side for those who like their steaks rare – longer for those who like them well done).

Arrange the steaks on a serving dish, surround with mashed potato and top with chicken and cream. Serve at once with a green vegetable or salad.

Herbed Stuffed Roast Chicken

Even if you don't have a garden, herbs in pots can now be bought with relative ease and grown on the kitchen window-sill. The effort of watering them every other day is well worth the reward of having your own fresh herbs rather than the dried varieties which really bear no relation to the subtlety of freshly-picked herbs. A good roasting chicken, preferably bought unfrozen, deserves such simple treatment as this.

Serves 4–6

3½ oz (100 g) butter
1 small onion
2 oz (50 g) fresh white breadcrumbs
1 tablespoon finely-chopped fresh sage
1 tablespoon finely-chopped fresh thyme
1 tablespoon finely-chopped tarragon
½ teaspoon finely-grated lemon peel
1 egg, beaten
Salt and freshly-ground black pepper
2½–3 lb (1·1–1·4 kg) chicken
1 tablespoon flour
½ pint (275 ml) chicken stock
¼ pint (150 ml) dry cider

Melt 2 oz (50 g) of butter. Peel and very finely chop the onion or shallot. Add the shallot or onion to the butter and cook over a low heat until soft and transparent. Remove from the heat and mix in the breadcrumbs, herbs, lemon peel and egg. Season with salt and pepper and use the mixture to stuff the bird.

Cover the bird with the remaining butter, softened, and place it upside down in a roasting dish. Cover with buttered foil and roast in a moderately hot oven (400° F, Reg 6) for 50 minutes, basting frequently with the juices in the pan. Remove the foil, turn the bird the right way up and brown for a further 10 minutes until the breast is golden brown.

Remove the chicken on to a serving dish. Put the roasting dish on top of the stove and spoon off excess fat. Add the flour to the juices in the pan. Mix well until the flour is browned and gradually blend in the stock and cider. Bring to the boil and boil hard until sauce is reduced to about two-thirds of the quantity. Serve the sauce separately.

Port Navas Jugged Duck with Oysters

The method of cooking poultry and game by 'jugging' it may be old-fashioned but it has nevertheless many advantages, going perhaps one step further than slow casserole cooking in the way it makes the best possible use of every bit of moisture and flavour in the ingredients. The mixture is cooked in a tall earthenware container (it is now possible to buy proper jugging vessels from some of the more sophisticated kitchen equipment shops but if you cannot get one of these, use an ordinary stoneware or earthenware jug and cover the top with foil).

Serves 6

1 duck with giblets
2 pints (1 litre) water
1 chicken stock cube
2 sprigs parsley
2 leaves sage
2 bay leaves
1 onion
2 carrots
Salt and freshly-ground black pepper
3 oz (75 g) butter
12 oysters

Joint the duck: cut off the legs at the joint. Cut off the wings flush to the body. Cut off the breasts in one piece from each side and cut each breast in half. Combine the gizzards, neck and heart with the water, stock cube, herbs and vegetables in a saucepan. Season with salt and pepper, bring to the boil and simmer for $1\frac{1}{2}$ hours. Strain well.

Cook the duck liver in $\frac{1}{2}$ oz (15 g) of the butter for 4 minutes, rub through a sieve and add to the duck stock. Dip the duck joints in seasoned flour and fry them in hot melted butter until well browned on all sides.

Pack half the duck joints in a high narrow vessel. Place

the oysters in a layer in the centre and pack the remaining duck joints in tightly.

Pour over the duck stock and cover tightly with foil. Place in a saucepan the height of the pot in which the duck is to be cooked but a little larger, and fill the pan with boiling water. Cook on top of the stove, keeping the water in the saucepan bubbling gently for 1 hour.

Turn out the jugged duck on to a serving dish and serve with potatoes and a green vegetable.

Braised Duck with Peas

Many people think of the traditional duck with peas combination as being merely a roast duck with green peas on the side. In fact I believe the duck in this traditional recipe should be par-roasted and then braised with the peas and a savoury addition of mint and sage. It is ideal for home-raised or free-range ducks that just might be a little on the tough side. Use rather large fresh peas rather than the smallest most tender ones.

Serves 4–5

1 duck with giblets
2 onions
4 fresh sage leaves
1 sprig mint
1 pint (575 ml) beef stock or water and $1\frac{1}{2}$ beef stock
    cubes
Salt and freshly-ground black pepper
1 lb (450 g) peas

Clean the duck and put the liver and 1 onion, peeled, in the cavity. Tie for roasting.

Roast the duck, without extra fat, in a moderately hot oven (400° F, Reg 6) for 30 minutes. Blanch the sage and mint leaves in boiling water for 2 minutes. Drain and place them in a large heavy pan with the other onion, peeled and quartered. Put in the duck, pour over the stock and season with salt and pepper. Bring to the boil and simmer for 15 minutes. Add the peas, bring to the boil, cover tightly and continue to cook for a further 25–30 minutes or until the peas and duck are tender.

Lift out the duck and place it on a serving dish. Lift out the peas, discarding the mint and sage leaves and the onion, and arrange them around the duck. Strain the liquid from the saucepan, skim off as much fat as possible from the surface and serve the gravy separately.

7

Cider and Apples

Cooking apples form the basis of many traditional, mouthmelting recipes whereas cider apples produce a golden draught that is a joy to drink; a harvest that, more than almost anything else, brings to mind the glory and the riches of the West of England.

ALTHOUGH the methods of making cider have inevitably been modernised at the Taunton Cider Company, and are now carried out on a grand scale with enormous vats storing the cider and lorries trundling in and out of the yards to distribute it around the country, the basic principles remain the same and many of the varieties of apple used in the making of the cider are as old as time itself.

In our walk through the orchards we were shown such trees as Porter's Perfection, Hangydown, Kingston Black and Slapma Girdle, only a few of the over 3,000 varieties available for blending together to make good cider that is far removed from the sweet, fizzy drink many people seem to associate with the name. The apples are gathered from both small and large orchards and it is still not unusual to see a farmer drive up to the brewery and unload just a few bags of apples from his boot. These will be weighed and then thrown on to the high mounds of other apples waiting to be crushed, pulped and squeezed through straw mats to extract the juices.

What most people don't seem to realise is that cider is stronger than beer. Scrumpy, the local rough cider made in Cornwall, Devon and Somerset, is very strong indeed, and soon has even the most hardened beer drinkers under the table if a large quantity is drunk.

As a cooking ingredient, cider has the same qualities as wine but at a much cheaper price. The taste of the apples also emerges during the cooking period and gives a good flavour to a great many dishes. At the Taunton Cider Company they recommend that, especially for sauces, the cider should be boiled first to reduce it.

Sausages and Onions in Cider

Serves 4

2 large onions
1½ oz (40 g) lard or dripping

8 pork sausages
¾ pint (425 ml) medium dry cider
½ oz (15 g) butter
1 tablespoon flour
Salt and freshly-ground black pepper
3 tablespoons cream
1 tablespoon finely-chopped parsley

Peel and thinly slice the onions and divide into rings. Heat the lard in a heavy frying pan, add the onions and cook over a low heat until soft and transparent. Remove the onions from the pan with a slotted spoon, add the sausages and cook over a medium-low heat, shaking the pan, until lightly browned on all sides. Strain off any excess fat and return the onions to the pan. Pour over the cider, cover tightly and simmer for 20 minutes. Strain off the liquid and keep the sausages and onions warm on a heated serving dish.

Melt the butter in a saucepan. Add the flour and mix well. Gradually add the cooking liquid, stirring continually over a medium-high heat until the sauce is thick and smooth. Season with salt and pepper, add the cream and parsley and pour the sauce over the sausages and onions.

Pork Fillet with Cider Sauce

Pork fillet is a great delicacy and, if treated like escallops of veal, can be stretched to make a luxury but reasonably-economical dinner party dish.

Serves 4

1¼ lb (575 g) pork fillet
Flour
Salt, freshly-ground black pepper and a pinch of paprika
1–2 oz (25–50 g) butter
1 large onion

6 oz (175 g) firm button mushrooms
$\frac{1}{2}$ pint (275 ml) dry cider
$\frac{1}{4}$ pint (150 ml) double cream
2 tablespoons finely-chopped parsley

Cut the pork into eight slices. Place the slices between two sheets of greaseproof paper and bash them with a meat mallet or rolling pin until they are no more than $\frac{1}{8}$ in (3 mm) thick. Peel the slices off the greaseproof paper and coat them with flour seasoned with salt, pepper and a little paprika.

Melt the butter in a heavy frying pan. Add the pork and cook over a high heat for $2\frac{1}{2}$ minutes on each side until the pork slices are just tender and golden brown on both sides. Remove with a slotted spoon and keep warm.

Peel and finely chop the onion. Thinly slice the mushrooms. Add the onion to the juices in the pan and cook over a low heat until soft and transparent. Add the mushrooms and continue to cook over a low heat for a further three minutes. Gradually add the cider, stirring continually until all the juices in the pan are amalgamated. Add the cream and pork slices and cook, without boiling for about 3 minutes.

Serve sprinkled with the parsley.

Pork Belly over Roast

Inexpensive but very good. The fat from the pork belly drips on to the vegetables, making them deliciously soft and well flavoured.

Serves 4

$2\frac{1}{2}$ lb (1·1 kg) pork belly in a piece
Coarse salt
$1\frac{1}{2}$ lb (675 g) potatoes
3 carrots
12 shallots, or onions cut into walnut-sized pieces

1½ tablespoons vegetable oil
½ pint (275 ml) brown stock or thin gravy
1 tablespoon redcurrant jelly
Pinch sage
Freshly-ground black pepper

Score the rind of the pork at ½-in (1-cm) intervals (use a sharp pointed knife and just cut through the rind). Rub the cuts with coarse salt.

Peel the potatoes and cut them into pieces the size of small eggs. Peel and roughly chop the carrots. Peel the shallots. Pour the oil into a roasting tin and arrange the vegetables in the bottom of the tin. Place a rack over the tin and put the belly, skin side up, on top. Roast in a moderately hot oven (400° F, Reg 6) for 1¾ hours or until the meat is cooked.

Combine the stock or gravy in a saucepan with the redcurrant jelly and heat through until the jelly has melted. Add the sage, season with salt and pepper and simmer for three minutes to allow the flavour of the sage to develop.

Put the meat on a warmed serving dish and surround with the vegetables; serve the sauce separately.

Somerset Pork Chops

A rich country-style dish that makes a good main course when the evenings begin to have a snap in the air.

Serves 4

4 pork chops
1 lb (450 g) cooking apples
1 large onion
1 tablespoon sugar
¼ pint (150 ml) dry cider
¼ teaspoon dried sage
¼ teaspoon dried savory
Salt and freshly-ground black pepper
4 tablespoons fresh white breadcrumbs

1½ oz (40 g) grated Cheddar cheese
2 oz (50 g) butter

Trim off surplus fat from the pork chops. Peel, core and slice the apples. Peel and finely chop the onion. Arrange the apple and onion in a lightly-greased fireproof dish, sprinkle with sugar and top with the chops. Pour over the cider. Sprinkle over the sage and savory and season.

Combine the breadcrumbs with the grated cheese and spread the mixture over the chops. Dot with butter and bake in a moderately hot oven (400° F, Reg 6) for 45 minutes or until the chops are tender.

Fried Sausages with Apples

Serves 4

1 lb (450 g) pork sausages (preferably the herby kind.
    Marks and Spencer produce a very good one)
Bacon fat
2 cooking apples
1½ lb (675 g) mashed potato
1 oz (25 g) butter
2 tablespoons cream
Salt, freshly-ground black pepper and a pinch nutmeg

Cook the sausages in a little bacon fat, without pricking them, over a low heat until cooked and well browned. Remove with a slotted spoon and keep warm.

Peel, core and slice the apples. Add the apples to the juices left from cooking the sausages (remove any excess fat) and cook over a low heat until tender.

Beat the potato with the butter and cream, season with salt and pepper and nutmeg and warm until hot through.

Arrange the potatoes in a circle around the outside of a serving dish and put the sausages in the centre surrounded by a ring of apples.

Casserole of Bacon Hock and Vegetables in Cider

Serves 6

1 bacon hock
1 small onion
1 bay leaf
Small sprig thyme
1 sage leaf
Salt and freshly-ground black pepper
1 pint (575 ml) cider
Water
2 carrots
1 large onion
1 turnip
2 oz (50 g) butter
1½ tablespoons flour
2 tablespoons cream
2 tablespoons finely-chopped parsley
3 tablespoons browned breadcrumbs

Put the bacon hock into a saucepan with the small onion, peeled and roughly chopped, the bay leaf, thyme and sage leaf. Season with pepper and add the cider. Put in enough water to cover, bring to the boil and cook for about 1 hour or until the bacon hock is tender. Strain off the liquid and leave the hock to cool.

Peel and chop the carrots. Peel and chop the onion. Peel and dice the turnip. Add the vegetables to the liquid in which the hock was cooked, bring to the boil and cook for about 20 minutes or until tender. Strain off and reserve the cooking liquid.

Remove the skin from the bacon hock and dice the flesh. Melt 1 oz (25 g) of butter in a saucepan. Add the flour and mix well. Gradually blend in the cooking liquid, stirring continually over a medium-high heat until the sauce is thick and smooth (there should be about a pint of liquid; if you need more add a little stock or water). Simmer the sauce for

3 minutes, check seasoning, mix in the cream and then add the vegetables and diced bacon. Mix in the parsley and turn into a casserole. Sprinkle the breadcrumbs over the top, dot with a little butter and cook in a moderately hot oven (375° F, Reg 5) for about 15 minutes until the top is crisp and the dish hot through.

Brisket Cooked in Cider

Serves 8–10

8 shallots
4 lb (1·8 kg) brisket of beef, rolled and tied
3 tablespoons black treacle
1 teaspoon pickling spice (this can be bought from Boots)
Herbs tied in a bunch (2 bay leaves, 3 sprigs parsley, sprig thyme, sprig marjoram)
$\frac{1}{4}$ pint (150 ml) red wine vinegar
Medium dry cider

Peel shallots. Put the meat in a flameproof casserole just large enough to hold it comfortably. Spread the meat with the treacle and pickling spice; smother with the shallots and the bunch of herbs. Pour over the wine, cover tightly with foil and leave to stand in a cool place for 24 hours.

Pour over enough cider to cover the meat and bring gently to the boil on top of the stove. Skim off any scum from the surface, cover tightly and simmer for about 3 hours until the meat is tender.

Honied Hocks

This is one of Vee's recipes – economical and very good indeed. Any leftover bacon can be made into delicious sandwiches.

On my frequent shopping visits to Plymouth I make a point of buying bacon hocks in the market. They come, I imagine, from the end of bacon joints and are a snip even at present-day prices. They are not particularly tidy to look at but they taste marvellous.

Serves 4

2 bacon hocks
2 tablespoons thick honey
2 oz (50 g) browned breadcrumbs
2 teaspoons made English mustard
Pinch ground cinnamon and ground cloves
$\frac{1}{4}$ pint (150 ml) cider

Cover the hocks with cold water, bring to the boil and simmer for about 2 hours until just tender. Remove from the cooking liquid (this can be used for stock if it is not too salty) and leave to cool. Carefully cut off the skin leaving as much fat as possible on the joints.

Heat the honey gently until melted. Mix with the breadcrumbs, mustard and spices and spread evenly all over the hocks. Put the hocks into a small baking tin and pour in the cider. Bake in a moderately hot oven (375° F, Reg 5) for 20 minutes or until browned and crisp.

Note: If you own a pressure cooker this is the ideal vessel for cooking the hocks.

Boiled Streaky Bacon with Broad Beans and Parsley Sauce

Serves 4

2 lb (900 g) streaky bacon in a piece
$\frac{1}{4}$ pint (150 ml) cider
2 lb (900 g) broad beans in the pod
1 small onion
1 oz (25 g) butter
2 tablespoons flour
$\frac{3}{4}$ pint (425 ml) milk

4 tablespoons finely-chopped parsley
Salt and freshly-ground black pepper

Put the bacon in a pan with the cider and just enough cold water to cover. Cover tightly and bring very slowly to the boil over a low flame. Simmer gently for 10 minutes, then remove the pan from the heat and leave to stand, in the cooking liquid, for a further fifteen minutes.

Pod the beans and cook them in boiling salted water until just tender (10–20 minutes depending on size). Drain well. Peel and finely chop the onion. Melt the butter in a saucepan, add the onion and cook over a low heat until soft and transparent. Add the flour, mix well and gradually blend in the milk, stirring continually over a medium-high heat until the sauce comes to the boil and is thick and smooth. Add the parsley, season with salt and pepper and simmer for three minutes. Mix in the beans.

Remove the bacon from the cooking liquid and cut into thin slices. Arrange the slices on a heated serving dish and surround with the beans in the parsley sauce.

8

A Miscellany of Savouries for Lunch, Supper or Light, Quick Meals

Memories of hearty breakfasts and high tea spreads; quick but satisfying meals for busy workers and appetising savoury delicacies.

Cheddar

THIS most famous of British cheeses comes from the West Country. Cheddar is still made throughout the Mendips in Somerset although, sadly, the traditional round shape is often replaced by large blocks these days because, I imagine, such shapes are more easily stored.

At one time enormous Cheddar cheeses were made in Somerset farmhouses. Often farmers pooled their milk together for this purpose with the prize, in the seventeenth century, going to those who made a cheese of around ten hundredweight. The standardisation of Cheddar cheese among the small cheese makers was brought about in the first half of the nineteenth century by a Joseph Harding. Later, Joseph's son went to Australia – hence the extremely good Australian and New Zealand cheeses now made there.

As is often the case these days with other things the flavour of Cheddar is frequently spoilt by the cheese being eaten before it is truly ripe. For perfection it should be allowed to stand for as much as a year before being eaten and, although you can sometimes buy 'mature' Cheddar, all too often it is sold within only a short time of having been made. To combat this, I have wrapped a small round Cheddar in a muslin cloth soaked in vinegar and kept it in the bottom of my refrigerator for three months. The flavour was very much improved, especially when the cheese was eaten at the end of dinner with Bath Oliver biscuits and crisp celery stalks.

As a cooking cheese, Cheddar is very good indeed – again you want to try and find a stronger cheese rather than a mild one. I tend to find that, for my taste anyway, most recipes specify the use of rather too little cheese in a dish. If you are going to flavour a dish with cheese, I feel it should have more than just a hint of a cheesy tang.

A little made English mustard helps to bring out the flavour of cheese in a dish; so does a little pale ale or dry cider. Cayenne, used with discretion, also complements a cheese flavour, nutmeg goes well in a cheese sauce and so do a few very finely chopped sage leaves. As a topping a layer of coarsely-grated cheese, put under a grill until it is a rich golden brown, melted and oozing, is delicious to finish off a plain country dish. The cheese can be mixed with breadcrumbs to make a crisper topping or spread over sliced potatoes to provide body to a dish. Small squares of Cheddar cheese also make a delightful alternative to croûtons of fried bread in clear vegetable soups.

Blue Vinney

The only other speciality cheese of the West Country is the Blue Vinney from Dorset. The real thing is now hard to find and most cheese bought under this name is like a rather second-grade Stilton.

Blue Vinney was made from milk skimmed by hand and the cheeses would be stored in a damp shed, often housing horse harnesses with a damp bloom on the leather that was conducive to forming the blue mould streaks that made the cheese special. Having been made and pressed into circular shapes, the cheese would be left to mature for at least eighteen months, and at the end of that time would be so hard it is said the people of Dorset sometimes used the round cheeses as wheels.

Farmhouse Cheeses

Cottage and cream cheeses are still produced on some farms, and it is good news to know that some dairies, like the Withiel dairy in Cornwall, are now reviving an interest in home-made country cheeses. In Somerset the art of producing *real* farmhouse cheese is rapidly gathering a following.

Cider Cheese Eggs

A quickly-made, warming supper dish.

Serves 4

1 large onion
1½ oz (40 g) butter
2 tablespoons flour
½ pint (275 ml) medium dry cider
2 oz (50 g) grated Cheddar cheese
Salt and freshly-ground black pepper
8 hard-boiled eggs
Pinch paprika pepper

Peel and thinly slice the onion and divide into rings. Melt half the butter in a saucepan. Add the onion and cook over a low heat until really soft and transparent. Transfer to a shallow serving dish. Melt the remaining butter, add the flour and mix well. Gradually blend in the cider, stirring continually over a medium-high heat until the sauce is thick and smooth. Bring to the boil, lower the heat, mix in the cheese and stir until it has melted. Season with salt and pepper.

Shell the eggs, cut each one in half and arrange them, cut side down, on top of the onions. Pour over the cheese sauce, sprinkle with a little paprika pepper and heat through in a moderate oven (400° F, Reg 6) for about 10 minutes before serving.

Pancakes with Cottage Cheese and Bacon

Light pancakes with a fresh country flavour. They can be
served as either a first or main course.

Serves 4–6

Pancakes:

4 oz (125 g) plain flour
Pinch salt
1 egg
½ pint (275 ml) milk
Olive oil

Filling:

4 thin rashers streaky bacon
2 tablespoons finely-chopped chives or spring onion
   tops
8 oz (225 g) cottage cheese
Salt and freshly-ground black pepper

Combine the flour with a pinch of salt, the egg and milk and
beat with a rotary or electric whisk until the batter is smooth.
Leave to stand for 30 minutes. Heat a little olive oil in an
omelette pan, swirling around until it begins to smoke.
Add about 2 tablespoons of batter, swirling it around the
pan over a high heat, until the bottom of the pan is coated
with a thin film of batter. Cook over a high heat for about 3
minutes until the pancake is lightly browned on the bottom
and set firm. Turn over and brown the other side. Slide the
pancake on to a plate and continue in the same way with the
rest of the batter. Stack the pancakes, one on top of another,
until all the batter has been used.

   Remove the rinds from the bacon and cut the rashers into
small pieces. Cook the bacon pieces with the rinds but
without any extra fat, until crisp and then discard the rinds.
Drain on kitchen paper. Combine the bacon and chives or

spring onion tops with the cottage cheese and season with salt and pepper.

Fill the pancakes with the cottage cheese mixture and roll up neatly. Arrange in a lightly-buttered baking dish and heat through in a moderately hot oven (400° F, Reg 6) for about 10 minutes.

Stilton Cream Cheese

    6 oz (175 g) Stilton cheese
    4 oz (125 g) cream cheese
    Freshly-ground black pepper
    Pinch cayenne and celery salt

Mash the Stilton until smooth and blend it with the cream cheese. Season with pepper, cayenne and celery salt, mix well and pile in a mound on a serving plate.

Serve the cheese with hot cream crackers.

Baked Eggs with Cheese

    Serves 4

    Butter
    2 oz (50 g) Cheddar cheese
    4 eggs
    4 tablespoons double cream
    1 tablespoon finely-chopped chives or spring onion tops
    Salt and pinch cayenne pepper

Butter four ramekin dishes. Cut cheese into very small dice and divide between the four dishes. Break an egg into each dish and pour over the cream mixed with the chives or spring onion tops. Sprinkle the top of each dish with a little salt and cayenne pepper and bake in a moderate oven (350° F, Reg 4) for about 10 minutes until the egg is just set.

Variations

Place a thick slice of tomato in the bottom of each dish before adding the cheese.
Combine the cheese with a little chopped ham.
Add a little made English mustard to the cream and chives.
Combine the cheese with a little chopped mushroom cooked in butter.

Flaggon Cheese

4 oz (125 g) Cheddar cheese
2 oz (50 g) softened butter
1 oz (25 g) cream cheese
2 tablespoons medium dry sherry
Pinch mace
Freshly-ground black pepper

Finely grate the Cheddar cheese and pound it with the butter and cream cheese until the mixture is quite smooth. Blend in the sherry and season with a little mace and freshly-ground black pepper.
Pack into a small dish or pot and keep in a refrigerator.

Note: This cheese can be served on hot toast with a poached egg on top as a light and quickly-prepared supper dish.

Potted Cheeses

Potted recipes are ideal for stretching small amounts of a basic ingredient and, in the case of cheese, using up the 'heels' of stale cheese that have gone hard and crusty. Serve potted cheese with cream crackers or salted biscuits that have been warmed in the oven to make them hot and crisp. Have a jar of crunchy celery stalks on the side.
Potted cheese can be covered with foil or plastic film and kept in a refrigerator for up to two weeks.

Potted Stilton

This can also be made in an electric mixer or liquidiser.

4 oz (125 g) Stilton cheese
4 oz (125 g) cream or cottage cheese
2 oz (50 g) softened butter
1 tablespoon brandy
2½ fl oz (75 ml) double cream
Pinch cayenne pepper

Crumble the cheese and mash it with a fork, or use a pestle and mortar, until smooth. Blend in the cottage or cream cheese and continue to beat until the mixture is smooth and well blended. Add the butter, brandy and cream and beat until light and well mixed. Season with a little cayenne and pack into a small dish or pot.

Potted Cheese with Herbs

The herbs in this recipe need to be *very* finely chopped or they overpower the taste of the cheese. This potted cheese should not be kept for more than 4 days, as although the flavour will develop nicely if it is kept longer the taste of the herbs is apt to become too strong.

6 oz (175 g) Cheddar or Cheshire cheese
3 tablespoons dry sherry
2 tablespoons double cream
Salt and freshly-ground black pepper
1 teaspoon finely-chopped parsley
¼ teaspoon finely-chopped sage
2 teaspoons finely-chopped thyme
2 teaspoons finely-chopped chives
1 teaspoon finely-chopped tarragon

Grate the cheese through the fine side of a grater. Combine the cheese, sherry and cream in a heavy saucepan and season with salt and pepper. Add the herbs and cook over a very low heat, stirring continually until the cheese has melted and the consistency is that of thick custard. Remove from the heat, cool and pack into an earthenware jar. Leave until quite cold and then store in a refrigerator until required.

Note: I serve this cheese as a savoury, sprinkled with a little cayenne pepper and accompanied by some hot salted cheese biscuits.

Scrumbled Cheese with Herbs

Spread on toast and grill quickly to serve as a savoury, spread on crisp biscuits or use as a sandwich filler.

>   4 oz (125 g) grated Cheddar cheese
>   3 tablespoons medium dry sherry
>   2 tablespoons double cream
>   2 tablespoons fresh, mixed, very finely-chopped chives, tarragon, parsley and sage
>   Salt, freshly-ground black pepper and a pinch cayenne

Pound the cheese with the sherry until the mixture is smooth. Blend in the cream and herbs and season with salt, freshly ground black pepper and a little cayenne. Pack into a small pot and chill in the refrigerator for at least two hours before serving.

The Duke's Mushroom Savoury

I am not sure who the 'Duke' was. This recipe is an adaptation of a recipe from the collection of an eighteenth-century Devon housekeeper. It can be served as a starter before a light main course, as a light lunch or supper dish or as a savoury to end a grand meal.

>   *Serves 4–6*
>
>   4 large 2-in (5-cm) thick slices white bread
>   2 chipples or spring onions

3 anchovy fillets
3 oz (75 g) butter
8 oz (225 g) firm button mushrooms
2 tablespoons finely-chopped parsley
1 teaspoon lemon juice
Freshly-ground black pepper and a pinch cayenne

Remove the crusts from the bread, cut each slice in half and then carefully make *croustades* by cutting three-quarters of the way through each rectangle, $\frac{1}{4}$ in (6 mm) from the outer edge. Remove the bread from the centre and leave a neat box-shaped receptacle.

Finely chop the chipples or spring onions. Very finely chop the anchovy fillets. Melt the butter in a frying pan and use some of it to brush the centre and sides of the bread cases.

Add the chipples and anchovies to the remaining butter and cook over a low heat, stirring to prevent sticking, for 3 minutes. Add the mushrooms and cook over a medium-high heat, tossing every now and then, for a further 4 minutes. Add parsley and lemon juice and season with a small pinch of cayenne and a generous twist of pepper. Mix lightly and divide between the bread cases.

Place the cases on a baking sheet and bake in a moderately hot oven (375° F, Reg 5) for about 15 minutes or until crisp and golden brown.

Creamed Mushrooms

Serves 6

12 oz (350 g) small, firm, button mushrooms
2 oz (50 g) butter
2 oz (50 g) flour
Salt, freshly-ground black pepper and a pinch of ground
    nutmeg
$\frac{1}{4}$ pint (150 ml) milk
$\frac{1}{4}$ pint (150 ml) double cream

4 thin slices white bread
Lard or clear dripping

Slice the mushrooms, having picked them over if necessary (you should only have to do this if the mushrooms are freshly-picked field mushrooms). Melt the butter in a saucepan, add the mushrooms and cook over a low heat for 5 minutes. Sprinkle over the flour. Mix lightly and cook for 2 minutes until the fat has been absorbed by the flour. Season with salt, pepper and a pinch of nutmeg and gradually add the milk, stirring gently over a low heat until the sauce comes to the boil and is thick and smooth. Continue to cook for 3 minutes to release the flavour of the mushrooms into the sauce, then remove from the heat and stir in the cream. Keep warm.

Remove the crusts from the bread and fry the slices in hot lard or dripping until golden brown. Drain on kitchen paper and top with the mushroom mixture. Serve at once.

Tawna Herb Bake

Herbs have always been put to good use in the West Country, particularly in Cornwall and Devonshire. There are herby pasties, herby pies – and this herb and batter mixture which makes a good light main course.

Serves 4

1 large bunch parsley
1 bunch watercress
¼ lb (125 g) turnip tops
1 crisp lettuce
4 spring onions or 1 tablespoon finely-chopped chives
4 borage leaves
¼ lb (125 g) spinach leaves
Salt and freshly-ground black pepper
2 eggs

5 tablespoons flour
$\frac{1}{2}$ pint (275 ml) milk

Cut off the tougher stems of the parsley, watercress and turnip tops. Remove the outer leaves of the lettuce and roughly shred the heart. Chop the spring onions. Put all the herbs and vegetables in a little boiling salted water and boil for 4 minutes. Put in a colander or sieve, drain well and press lightly to remove all the excess water. Arrange in a lightly-greased baking dish and season well with salt and pepper.

Beat the eggs with the flour and milk until smooth. Season with salt and pepper, pour the batter over the leaves, mix well and bake in a moderate oven (350° F, Reg 4) until the batter is well risen, crisp and a pale golden colour.

Serve at once.

Maidenwell Potato Cakes

Serves 6

$1\frac{1}{2}$ lb (675 g) new potatoes
$\frac{1}{2}$ oz (15 g) butter
4 tablespoons flour
1 shallot or small onion
4 tablespoons finely and freshly-grated Parmesan cheese
1 tablespoon finely-chopped parsley
Salt and freshly-ground black pepper
2 well-beaten eggs
Fine dry breadcrumbs
Olive or vegetable oil for frying

Wash the potatoes and boil them in their skins until just tender. Drain, peel when cold enough to handle and mash until smooth with the butter and flour. Peel and finely chop the shallot or onion. Mix the onion, cheese and parsley into the potato, season with salt and pepper and beat in the eggs.

Mix well and, using floured hands, shape into $\frac{1}{2}$-in (1-cm) thick cakes, 2 in (5 cm) across.

Coat in breadcrumbs and fry until crisp and golden in very hot oil. Drain on kitchen paper.

Egg and Asparagus Ramekins

The timing for baked eggs is always tricky. When in doubt take out the eggs while still a little runny – they go on cooking after they have been removed from the oven because of the heat retained by the pots.

Serves 4

$1\frac{1}{2}$ oz (40 g) butter
3 oz (75 g) cooked asparagus
1 teaspoon finely-chopped parsley
2 tablespoons cream
Salt and freshly-ground black pepper
4 eggs

Use $\frac{1}{4}$ oz (7 g) of butter to grease four ramekin dishes. Chop the cooked asparagus and stew it in the remaining butter until it is really soft. Strain off the butter into a bowl and mix in the parsley and cream; season with a little salt and pepper. Divide the asparagus between the four ramekins. Break an egg over each bed of asparagus. Pour over the butter mixture, cover with foil and bake in a moderate oven (350° F, Reg 4) for 8–10 minutes until the yolk is just set.

Note: Some recipes call for asparagus tips only, and the leftover stalks are ideal for use in this dish.

Pickled Eggs

This home-made recipe is well worth trying and the eggs make a good standby for summer picnics or salad meals.

16 eggs
½ oz (15 g) piece of ginger root
2 pints (1 litre) vinegar
½ oz (15 g) black peppercorns
½ oz (15 g) allspice

Hard-boil the eggs for 10 minutes, plunge them immediately into cold water and shell when cold.

Bruise the ginger by crushing it. Combine the vinegar with the peppercorns, allspice and bruised ginger. Bring to the boil and simmer for 10 minutes. Leave until cold.

Place the eggs in a sterilised jar just large enough to take them and pour over the vinegar, filling the jar to the brim. Seal and leave in a cool dark place for 4 weeks before opening.

Devonshire Dish of Bacon with Fried Cooked Potatoes

It was an old Devonshire custom to cook enough potatoes one day to fry with the bacon for the next morning's breakfast.

Serves 4

8 very thin rashers streaky bacon
1½ tablespoons bacon fat or dripping
1 lb (450 g) mashed potato
Salt and freshly-ground black pepper

Cook the bacon rashers in bacon fat or dripping until they are nicely crisp. Remove them from the pan and keep warm. Add the potatoes to the fat in the pan, season with salt and pepper and stir for 1 minute over a high heat. Press the potatoes down firmly in the pan and continue to cook until the potatoes are crisp and brown underneath.

Invert the potatoes on to a serving plate and top with the crisply-fried bacon rashers.

Bacon Pancakes

Serves 4

4 rashers bacon
3 oz (75 g) plain flour
$\frac{1}{2}$ teaspoon baking powder
3 tablespoons milk
1 tablespoon finely-chopped parsley
Pepper
Lard, vegetable oil or dripping for frying

Remove bacon rinds and finely chop rashers. Fry with the rinds but without extra fat until bacon is crisp. Drain bacon, remove rinds and reserve 1 teaspoon bacon fat.

Combine flour and baking powder and mix to a thick cream with the milk. Add the bacon and parsley and season with pepper.

Heat fat or oil. Add tablespoons of the pancake mixture and cook over a moderately-high heat until the cakes are golden brown on both sides.

Serve with fried eggs and grilled tomatoes, or in place of potatoes as a vegetable dish.

Ham and Egg Patties

In the good old days patties seem to have been any form of case upon which other ingredients were put. In this case the patty was a slice of fried bread, topped with a savoury mixture of minced ham and finished off with a poached egg on top. It makes an ideal supper dish, quickly produced and satisfying enough as a main course.

Serves 4

4 thick slices of white bread, crusts removed
Oil or lard for frying
1 small onion
8 oz (225 g) ham
1 oz (25 g) butter
$\frac{1}{2}$ teaspoon flour
$\frac{1}{4}$ pint (150 ml) stock
$\frac{1}{2}$ teaspoon lemon juice
2 tablespoons double cream
Pinch cayenne pepper
4 eggs

Cut an incision $\frac{1}{4}$ in (6 mm) from the edges of each slice of
bread, three-quarters of the way through the slice. Remove
the bread from the centre of the slice leaving a shallow bread
case. (This process can be skipped if you are in a hurry; it
looks nice and makes the dish a little more sophisticated but
isn't really necessary.) Fry the bread slices in hot oil or lard
until crisp and golden brown. Drain well on kitchen paper.
  Peel and very finely chop the onion. Mince the ham. Melt
the butter, add the onion and cook over a low heat until soft
and transparent. Add the flour, raise the heat and stir until
the flour is lightly browned. Gradually blend in the stock,
stirring continually until the sauce is thick and smooth. Add
the ham, mix well and blend in the lemon juice and cream.
Season with cayenne pepper.
  Poach the eggs in barely-boiling water until just set (about
4 minutes).
  Pile the ham mixture on the fried bread and top each slice
with a poached egg. Serve at once.

Tricolour Eggs

A delicious starter with a difference. Serve it on a hot summer
day and you have something as pleasurable to look at as it is
to eat.

Serves 4

¾ pint (425 ml) thick home-made mayonnaise
¼ teaspoon strand saffron
1 small shallot
½ tablespoon olive oil
½ tablespoon tomato purée
Handful sorrel or spinach leaves
4 sprigs parsley
Salt and freshly-ground black pepper
1 tablespoon double cream
Crisp lettuce leaves
6 hard-boiled eggs
6 anchovy fillets

Divide the mayonnaise into three portions. Pour one table-spoon of boiling water over the saffron and leave for 10 minutes. Strain off the liquid and leave to cool.

Peel and very finely chop the shallot. Heat the olive oil in a small saucepan, add the shallot and cook over a low heat until soft and completely transparent. Add the tomato purée and mix well; stir over a low heat for 2 minutes. Leave to cool.

Remove the stalks from the sorrel or spinach and the parsley and cook in boiling, salted water until parsley is just tender. Drain well, pressing out all excess liquid. Purée through a fine sieve or food mill and leave to cool.

Add the yellow saffron water and cream to one portion of mayonnaise, the red tomato mixture to another and the green herb purée to the third. Check all three for seasoning.

Arrange a bed of shredded lettuce leaves on four plates and top each bed with three hard-boiled egg halves placed cut side down. Mask the eggs with the three different kinds of mayonnaise and top each egg with half an anchovy fillet cut lengthwise down the middle. Serve chilled.

Ham Paste

If you cook a whole piece of ham or gammon on the bone, this is a useful way to use up those untidy trimmings of ham that remain at the end of the carving. The paste can be served as a first course or used as a sandwich filling.

2 large onions
1 lb (450 g) cooked ham or gammon
6 oz (175 g) butter
$\frac{1}{4}$ pint (150 ml) dry cider
Salt and freshly-ground black pepper
Pinch cayenne pepper
$\frac{1}{4}$ teaspoon paprika pepper
Pinch mace and ground nutmeg
Pinch finely-chopped sage

Peel and roughly chop the onions. Pass the ham through the coarse blades of a mincing machine. Melt 2 oz (50 g) of butter in a heavy frying pan. Add the onions and cook over a low heat until soft and transparent. Remove from the heat, add the ham, cider and another 2 oz (50 g) of butter, season with salt and pepper, the spices and sage. Mix well and either pound to a paste in a mortar or put in a liquidiser or through a food mill.

Pack into small jars and seal with clarified butter, brought to the boil and strained through a piece of muslin.

Potted Salmon

This is delicious to serve with toast as a first course or to use as a very superior filling for sandwiches.

$\frac{1}{2}$ lb (225 g) salmon cut off the bone and skinned
$\frac{1}{4}$ pint (150 ml) white wine
$2\frac{1}{2}$ fl oz (75 ml) water
2 sprigs parsley
1 small onion

1 bay leaf
Salt and freshly-ground black pepper
Pinch mace and ground nutmeg
4 oz (125 g) butter

Put the skin and bones of the salmon in a small saucepan
with the white wine, water, parsley, onion (peeled and
sliced) and the bay leaf. Season with salt and pepper and
bring to the boil, cover tightly and cook for $\frac{1}{2}$ hour over a
high heat. Strain off the liquid into a clean pan and boil fast
until reduced to half the quantity.

Place the salmon in a small earthenware pot. Pour in the
reduced liquid, add a little mace and nutmeg, cover with
foil so that no air can escape and bake in a moderate oven
(350° F, Reg 4) for 30 minutes or until the salmon is just
tender.

Beat the salmon and juice with 3 oz (75 g) of melted
butter until smooth. (Use a wooden spoon, pass through a
food mill or purée in a liquidiser.) Check seasoning, adding
more if necessary – the salmon should be rather on the
highly-seasoned side. Press firmly into a small jar and cover
with melted butter strained through a piece of muslin.

Potted Sprats

Serves 4

1 lb (450 g) sprats
Salt and freshly-ground black pepper
Pinch mace
5 oz (150 g) butter

Remove the heads and tails of the sprats and clean them.
Lay them in a well-greased dish, season with salt, plenty of
pepper and a pinch of mace and pour over the melted
butter. Cover very tightly with two layers of foil and bake
in a moderate oven (350° F, Reg 4) for 1–1$\frac{1}{2}$ hours until the
sprats are completely soft and the bones have melted.

Remove the sprats and pound them to a paste in a mortar, rub through a coarse sieve or force through a food mill. Beat the butter and cooking juices from the dish they were cooked in into the puréed sprats, check seasoning and pack tightly into small pots. Chill in a refrigerator. Serve with hot toast and quarters of lemon.

Potted Shrimps

Potted shrimps seemed to have been popular throughout England all through the eighteenth and nineteenth centuries. Spicings vary, but mace was always included and I myself very much like the inclusion of ground nutmeg. Whatever your flavourings, potted shrimps or prawns are always served with either brown bread and butter or hot toast, and accompanied by quarters of lemon.

Potted shrimps or prawns were often used as the basis of a sauce to go with fish. The shrimps were melted in a pan, flour was added and then enough milk to make a sauce. Chopped parsley can be added to the sauce.

The dish sounds extravagant for 4 because you strain off the cooking butter, but it's worth doing properly and the strained butter can be used to make the basis of a fish sauce.

Serves 4

6 oz (175 g) butter
8 oz (225 g) peeled shrimps or prawns
Salt and freshly-ground black pepper
$\frac{1}{4}$ teaspoon mace
$\frac{1}{4}$ teaspoon ground nutmeg
Pinch cayenne

Melt 4 oz (125 g) butter. Add shrimps or prawns, season with salt, pepper, mace and nutmeg, cover tightly and stew for 40 minutes over a *low* heat, stirring every now and then to prevent browning.

Remove from the heat, strain off the juices and pack the

shrimps tightly in a small earthenware jar. Melt remaining 2 oz (50 g) of butter and strain over the shrimps or prawns through a sieve lined with a piece of muslin.

Sprinkle with a little cayenne pepper and chill in a refrigerator.

Sauce from the strained butter

Heat butter in a pan. Add 2 tablespoons flour and mix well. Gradually blend in ¾ pint (425 ml) of milk, stirring continually over a medium-high heat until the sauce comes to the boil and is thick and smooth. Add 1 tablespoon finely-chopped chives and 1 of finely-chopped parsley and stir in 2 tablespoons double cream just before serving.

For a richer sauce blend in 1 tablespoon of sherry before adding the cream.

Potted Tongue

Potted meats can be served instead of pâté at the beginning of a meal, or they make delicious sandwich fillings.

>   8 oz (225 g) cooked ox tongue
>   Pinch nutmeg, ginger, mace and thyme
>   1 small clove garlic
>   6 oz (175 g) butter
>   Salt and freshly-ground black pepper

Pass half the tongue through the fine blades of a mincing machine.

Combine the spices, thyme and garlic clove in a mortar and pound with a pestle until the thyme is almost powdered and the garlic amalgamated with the other ingredients.

Combine 4 oz (125 g) of butter with the minced tongue and the spice mixture and mix to a smooth paste. Cut the remaining tongue into very small dice and mix it with the paste, seasoning with salt and pepper. Pack in a small dish.

Clarify the remaining butter by bringing it to the boil and

straining it through a piece of muslin. Pour the hot butter over the potted tongue and leave to cool.

Note: This can be kept in a refrigerator for up to three weeks.

Potted Salt Beef

A small amount of leftover boiled salt beef makes an excellent potted meat to serve with toast or on sandwiches.

8 oz (225 g) cooked salt beef
6 oz (175 g) butter
Freshly-ground black pepper and a pinch mace

Cut the beef into small pieces and then chop it finely (this can be done in an automatic chopper, but do not put through a mincing machine or into a liquidiser as this will destroy the texture of the meat).

Melt the butter in a saucepan, heat through until foaming and remove from the heat before it begins to brown. Strain through a piece of muslin to clarify it. Combine the butter with the meat and mix well. Season with pepper and a small pinch of mace and pack in a small earthenware dish or terrine.

The potted meat can be stored in a refrigerator for up to a week.

9

The Goodness of the Soil

*Britain produces some of the finest vegetables in Europe:
here is how to make the best possible use of this bounty.*

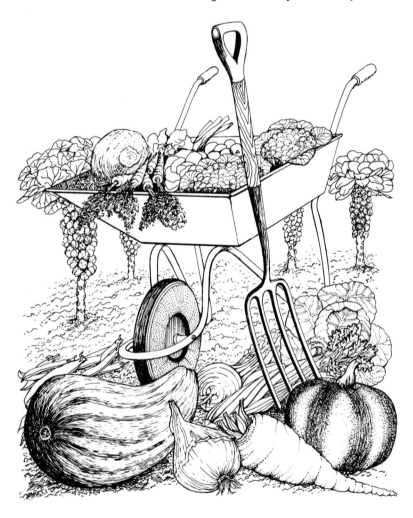

THE FIRST new potatoes in Cornwall are one of the most delicious things ever. Each year one forgets how delicious they taste and how, almost miraculously, their skins can be stripped off with a thumb nail.

At first we revel in the taste of the young tubers served as plain as possible, merely lightly boiled with a sprig or two of mint, tossed in butter with a sprinkling of freshly-ground black pepper and some finely-chopped parsley. As the season progresses I become more adventurous again, sautéing the whole new potatoes in butter or experimenting with a variety of delicious potato salads.

Hot Potato Salad with Anchovies and Bacon

This is one of those useful vegetable dishes that is good in its own right and perfectly adequate for a light lunch dish.

Serves 4

1½ lb (675 g) new potatoes
4 thin rashers streaky bacon
4 tablespoons olive oil
1 tablespoon white wine vinegar
½ teaspoon made English mustard
Freshly-ground black pepper
4 fillets anchovies
1 tablespoon finely-chopped parsley
1 tablespoon finely-chopped chives

Scrape the potatoes and boil them in salted water until just cooked. Drain, cool and cut into neat dice.

Remove the rind from the bacon and chop the rashers. Cook over a low heat until cooked through and crisp.

Combine the olive oil, vinegar and mustard, season with pepper and mix well. Chop the anchovy fillets.

Put the potatoes into a saucepan with the bacon and bacon fat, add the anchovies and dressing and toss over a moderate heat for just long enough to heat the ingredients. Add the parsley and chives, toss lightly to mix and serve at once.

Somerset Cream of Potatoes and Parsnips with Cabbage

Serves 4

1 lb (450 g) potatoes
½ lb (225 g) parsnips
Salt and freshly-ground black pepper and a pinch ground nutmeg
½ lb (225 g) firm cabbage
3 tablespoons milk or cream
1 oz (25 g) butter

Peel the potatoes and parsnips and boil them together in salted water until they are tender. Drain well. Remove the tough stem of the cabbage and cook in a little boiling salted water until tender. Drain well and chop finely. Mash the potatoes and parsnips with the milk and butter until smooth. Mix in the cabbage.

Season with salt and pepper and nutmeg, heat through and pile on to a serving dish.

New Potato Salad with Mint and Orange

Use only the very new potatoes and choose those that are not over the size of a walnut.

Serves 4

1½ lb (675 g) new potatoes
6 tablespoons olive oil
1½ tablespoons white wine vinegar
½ teaspoon made English mustard
1 tablespoon orange juice
1 tablespoon finely-chopped fresh mint

1 tablespoon finely-chopped chives
Salt and freshly-ground black pepper

Scrape the potatoes and boil them in salted water until just tender.

Combine the olive oil, vinegar, mustard, orange juice, mint and chives, season generously with salt and pepper and shake to mix well. Pour the dressing over the potatoes while they are still warm and toss lightly. Leave to cool.

New Potatoes with Cucumber Sticks in Cream

Serves 4

1 lb (450 g) new potatoes
1 small cucumber
4 leaves mint
4 tablespoons cream
Salt and freshly-ground black pepper

Scrape potatoes and cook in salted water until *just* tender.

Peel cucumber and cut into sticks about $\frac{1}{4}$ in (6 mm) thick and 1 in ($2\frac{1}{2}$ cm) long. Very finely chop mint. Heat cream in a saucepan without boiling. Add potatoes, cucumber and mint and season with salt and a generous twist of pepper.

Heat through and serve at once.

Baked White Turnip Pudding

This pie made of white turnips (the early variety) is both delicious and very warming on a cold day.

$1\frac{1}{2}$ lb (675 g) white turnips
Milk
3 tablespoons double cream
Salt and freshly-ground black pepper
1 oz (25 g) butter
2 oz (50 g) fresh white breadcrumbs
$1\frac{1}{2}$ oz (40 g) grated Cheddar cheese

Peel and dice the turnips, place in a saucepan, pour over enough milk to cover and cook until just tender. Drain off any excess milk and mash until smooth with the cream and a generous seasoning of salt and pepper.

Melt the butter and mix with the breadcrumbs and grated cheese. Spoon the turnips into a lightly-greased fireproof baking dish and cover with the breadcrumb mixture. Bake in a moderate oven (350° F, Reg 4) for 30 minutes.

Purée of Swede with Bacon

Serves 6

1 large swede
1 onion
2 rashers thin streaky bacon
1 oz (25 g) butter
2 tablespoons double cream
Salt and freshly-ground black pepper

Peel and dice the swede, cover it with cold water, add a pinch of salt and cook until tender. Drain well and mash until completely smooth.

Peel and finely chop the onion. Remove the rinds from the bacon and fry the rashers without extra fat until crisp. Drain on kitchen paper and crumble into small pieces. Add the onion to the bacon fat in the pan and cook over a low heat until soft and transparent.

Combine the mashed swede and onions in a clean pan. Add the butter and cream and mix well. Season with salt and pepper, stir to prevent sticking and cook until hot through.

Pile the mashed swede on to a serving dish and top with crisp bacon before serving.

Note: This dish is also delicious if it is made with equal quantities of swede and potato.

Mashed Parsnips with Cheese

Serves 4

1½ lb (675 g) parsnips
1½ oz (40 g) butter
2 tablespoons double cream
½ teaspoon dry mustard
Salt and freshly-ground black pepper
2 oz (50 g) finely-grated fresh white breadcrumbs
2 oz (50 g) grated cheese
½ oz (15 g) butter

Peel and roughly chop the parsnips and boil them in salted water until just tender. Drain well and mash until smooth. Beat in the butter and cream. Mix in the mustard and season with salt and pepper. Beat until the mixture is smooth.

Arrange half the parsnips in a buttered baking dish. Sprinkle with half the breadcrumbs and cheese and spread over the remaining parsnips. Top with the remaining breadcrumbs mixed with the cheese that is left, dot with butter and bake in a hot oven (425° F, Reg 7) for about 20 minutes until the top is golden brown (or put under a medium hot grill until the dish is browned on top and warmed through).

Sweedie Cake

Serves 6

1 large swede
1 onion
2 oz (50 g) butter
Salt and freshly-ground black pepper
Pinch nutmeg
1 tablespoon chopped parsley

Peel the swede, cut into sticks about 1½ in (4 cm) square and then into thin slices. Peel and finely chop the onion.

Melt the butter in a heavy frying pan. Add the onion and

cook over a low heat until soft and transparent. Remove with a slotted spoon and turn off the heat.

Arrange half the swede slices in the pan, season with salt, pepper and a pinch of nutmeg and spread over the onions. Arrange the remaining swede slices on top and season the layer. Cover with a large saucepan lid and cook over a low heat for about 30 minutes until the swede is cooked through.

Invert on to a serving dish and sprinkle with chopped parsley before serving.

BROAD BEANS

If you grow your own broad beans you have many more joys than just eating the shelled beans when they reach maturity. The tops, for instance, when they have to be nipped off to make the beans grow well, are delicious boiling-leaves, stalks, flowers and all. Treat like spinach, but be careful about seasoning as the bean tops are naturally salty from the minerals in the earth.

Those who are impatient for the new season's taste of broad beans, like me, can also try eating the small young pods whole, instead of waiting until the beans have matured. The very young beans, about 2 in (5 cm) long, can be boiled whole; those that are slightly longer (up to six inches (15 cm) providing the beans are still basically un-formed) can be cut into 1 in (2½-cm) lengths.

The fully-matured beans can be cooked, skinned and used in a salad; or they are delicious uncooked when they have a delicious crunchy texture and nutty flavour.

Large, tough, beans should be cooked, skinned and then puréed. The beans do not freeze all that well so it is well worth while making the best of the fresh produce for the short season they are available.

Broad Beans and Bacon

The broad bean and bacon combination is a well-tried one. In the summer, when the beans first swell on the pods and are small, sweet and tender, mixing them with a little bacon provides a light meal for a hot summer day. If you grow your own beans it is also most satisfactorily economical.

Serves 4

1 lb (450 g) young, shelled broad beans
$\frac{1}{2}$ lb (225 g) bacon in a piece
1$\frac{1}{2}$ oz (40 g) butter
Salt and freshly-ground black pepper
1 tablespoon finely-chopped parsley

Cook the beans in boiling salted water until just tender. Drain well and keep warm. Cover the bacon with cold water, bring to the boil and simmer for about 30 minutes until tender. Remove from water and cut into small dice.

Melt butter in a saucepan. Add beans and bacon, season with salt and pepper, add parsley, toss lightly and serve.

Beans and Bacon in Cream Sauce

Serves 4

1 lb (450 g) young, shelled broad beans
2 rashers streaky bacon
$\frac{1}{2}$ oz (15 g) butter
1 tablespoon flour
$\frac{1}{2}$ pint (275 ml) milk
1 tablespoon finely-chopped parsley
Salt and freshly-ground black pepper

Cook beans in boiling salted water until tender and drain. Remove the rinds of the bacon and chop the rashers. Cook the bacon without extra fat over a medium heat until cooked.

Melt the butter with the fat from the cooked bacon. Add the flour and mix well. Gradually add the milk, stirring continually over a medium-high heat until the sauce comes to the boil and is thick and smooth. Mix in the beans, bacon and parsley, season with salt and pepper, heat and serve.

Broad Beans in a Cream Sauce with Ham and Onions

So good it can be served as a main course. Savory is a herb traditionally served with broad beans.

Serves 4

2 lb (900 g) broad beans
$\frac{3}{4}$ pint (425 ml) milk
Sprig of savory
1 small onion
1 oz (25 g) butter
2 tablespoons flour
2 tablespoon finely-chopped parsley
2 oz (50 g) lean ham
$\frac{1}{4}$ pint (150 ml) double cream
Salt, freshly-ground black pepper and nutmeg

Shell the broad beans and cook them until just tender in boiling salted water. Combine the milk and sprig of savory, bring to the boil, simmer for 10 minutes. Strain the milk.

Peel and finely chop the onion.

Melt the butter in a saucepan. Add the onion and cook over a low heat until soft and transparent. Add the flour and mix well. Gradually add the hot milk, stirring continually over a medium-high heat until the sauce comes to the boil and is thick and smooth. Continue to boil the sauce, stirring all the time, for a further 3 minutes.

Add the beans, parsley and ham, mix in cream, season with salt, pepper and a touch of ground nutmeg and heat through without boiling.

Salad of Broad Beans

Use the older broad beans for this salad. You may find the
tough skins need peeling off, but the crunchy texture of the
beans makes this well worth while.

Serves 4

1 lb (450 g) large, shelled broad beans
2 rashers streaky bacon
3 tablespoons olive oil
½ teaspoon dry English mustard
1 tablespoon white wine vinegar
Salt and freshly-ground black pepper
3 spring onions

Cook beans in boiling salted water until tender, drain
well and leave to cool. Remove the rinds of the bacon and
finely chop the rashers. Cook the bacon without extra fat
over a medium-high heat until crisp, drain off fat and lay
bacon on kitchen paper.

Combine olive oil, mustard and vinegar in a screw-top jar,
season with salt and pepper and shake to mix well.

Peel off the shells of the broad beans. Finely chop the
spring onions. Combine the beans, bacon, onion and dressing, mix lightly and turn into a serving dish. Sprinkle with
parsley and serve chilled.

Note: This salad makes an adequate hot weather main course
if it is served with a green and tomato salad and some crusty
home-made bread.

RUNNER BEANS

Firm young runner beans should, to my way of thinking,
have nothing done to them at all except to be thinly sliced,
quickly boiled and served rather on the crisp, slightly-
undercooked side with plenty of butter and freshly-ground

---

black pepper. Older beans may need more fancy treatment, or they can make a good addition to soups and stews.

Runner Beans with Pears

Cider vinegar is used once again in this dish, to make a deliciously sweet/sour partner to boiled meat or ham.

    1 lb (450 g) runner beans
    4 firm eating pears
    ¾ pint (425 ml) good white stock
    Grated rind ½ lemon
    4 rashers streaky bacon
    2 teaspoons brown sugar
    1½ tablespoons cider vinegar
    Salt and freshly-ground black pepper

Remove the strings from the beans and cut into ½-in (1-cm) slices. Peel and quarter the pears and scoop out the cores. Bring the stock to the boil, add the lemon rind and drop in the pears. Cook over a low heat for 20 minutes, then add the beans and cook for a further 20 minutes until the beans are just tender (they should still maintain a slight crispness). Remove from the stock.

Fry the bacon, without extra fat, until crisp. Drain on kitchen paper, cut off the rinds and crumble the rashers. Add the sugar and vinegar to the bacon fat in the frying pan and stir until the sugar has dissolved. Blend in a few tablespoons of the stock and mix well. Add the sauce to the pears and beans. Season with salt and pepper, turn into a serving dish and top with the crumbled bacon.

Runner Beans with Tomatoes and Cheese

Serves 4

    1 lb (450 g) runner beans
    3 large, ripe tomatoes

1 onion
1 clove garlic
1 tablespoon olive oil
1 tablespoon tomato purée
Salt and freshly-ground black pepper
½ teaspoon finely-chopped savory
2 oz (50 g) grated Cheddar cheese
2 tablespoons fresh white breadcrumbs

String and slice the runner beans. Cover the tomatoes with boiling water for 2 minutes, slide off the skins and roughly chop the flesh. Peel and finely chop the onion. Peel and finely chop the garlic.

Heat the olive oil in a saucepan, add the onion and garlic and cook over a low heat until the onion is soft and transparent. Add the tomatoes and tomato purée, mix well, season with salt and pepper, add the savory, bring to the boil and simmer for 20 minutes.

Cook the beans in boiling salted water until just tender. Arrange in a lightly-buttered baking dish and pour over the sauce. Top with the cheese and the breadcrumbs mixed together and bake in a moderately hot oven (375° F, Reg 5) for about 20 minutes or until the top of the dish is crisp and golden brown.

French Beans with Mustard and Cream

Serves 4–6

1 lb (450 g) French beans
4 tablespoons single cream
2 teaspoons Urchart Wiltshire mustard

Top and tail the beans and cook them in a little boiling salted water until just tender. Drain well. Combine the cream and mustard in a clean saucepan and mix well. Heat through, add the beans and toss lightly until the beans are coated with the cream and mustard mixture.

Note: Urchart mustard is made in Wiltshire according to an old recipe and can be found in many delicatessen shops. It is a grainy mustard with whole seeds and deliciously piquant.

Braised Leeks with Bacon and Parsley

Serves 4

> 2 thin rashers bacon
> 12 young leeks
> 1 oz (25 g) butter
> ¼ pint (150 ml) stock (or water and ½ chicken stock cube)
> 4 tablespoons finely-chopped parsley

Remove the bacon rinds and finely chop the rashers. Clean the leeks, leaving them whole.

Heat the butter in a frying pan. Add the bacon and cook over a low heat for 10 minutes.

Arrange the leeks in a fireproof baking dish. Add the bacon and butter and pour over the stock mixed with the parsley. Cover with foil and bake in a moderate oven (350° F, Reg 4) for 30–45 minutes until the leeks are tender.

Leeks with Cream

I have had this made with clotted cream, but found it to be just a bit too rich.

Serves 4

> 4 large leeks
> Scant ¼ pint (125 ml) single cream
> Salt and freshly-ground black pepper
> 4 tablespoons dried breadcrumbs (preferably home-
>   made – very easy and so much nicer)
> ½ oz (15 g) butter

Clean the leeks and cook them in boiling water until tender. Drain well, placing them upside down in a colander so that all the liquid runs out. Place in a lightly-buttered baking dish.

Pour the cream over the leeks, season with salt and pepper and sprinkle over the breadcrumbs. Dot with small pieces of butter and cook in a moderately hot oven (375° F, Reg 5) for 15 minutes or until the dish is bubbling and the top golden brown.

Chipples, Chibbles or Spring Onions

If you ask for spring onions in a small-town Cornish or Devon grocer's you may well get a blank look or be told firmly that what you really mean is 'chipples' or 'chibbles' m'dear.

Chipples is the word in Cornwall, chibbles in Devon, and although both really refer to young shallots, the terms are also used for anything that resembles a spring onion as the rest of the world knows it.

The taste of cooked chipples is somewhat between that of young leeks and onions. Both the green as well as the white parts of the plants are used and they make a pleasant addition to many hot dishes as well as being an almost essential ingredient of a spring and early-summer salad.

Chipples and chibbles are used a lot in West Country cooking, sliced lengthwise and not chopped. They can also be used instead of chives and, all round, provide a cheap and satisfactory flavouring ingredient.

Beetroot and Chipple Salad

Serves 4

1 medium cooked beetroot
4 chipples or spring onions
3 tablespoons olive oil
1 teaspoon white wine vinegar

Salt, freshly-ground black pepper and a pinch allspice
1 tablespoon finely-chopped parsley

Skin the beetroot and cut the flesh into small dice. Clean and finely chop the chipples. Combine the beetroot and chipples in a glass dish. Mix the oil and vinegar and season with salt, pepper and a pinch allspice. Mix the parsley into the dressing, pour it over the salad ingredients and toss lightly.

Chill in a refrigerator until ready to serve.

Baked Shallots

Serves 4

1½ pints (875 ml) medium sweet cider
2 lb (900 g) shallots
Salt and freshly-ground black pepper
1 tablespoon soft brown sugar
4 oz (125 g) raisins

Put the cider into a saucepan, bring to the boil and boil hard until reduced to about one-third of the quantity (this will bring out the flavour of the cider).

Wash the shallots, put them in a saucepan, cover with cold water and bring to the boil. Drain off the water, leave shallots to cool and then remove the skins. Place the shallots in a well-buttered baking dish and season with salt and pepper. Mix the sugar with the cider, pour the liquid over the shallots, add the raisins, cover with foil and bake in a moderate oven (350° F, Reg 4) for about 30 minutes or until shallots are tender.

The dish can be served hot with roast meat or left to get cold, when it is very good with any cold meat.

Stuffed Spring Cabbage

Tender rugby-football-shaped cabbages are very much a feature of the West Country spring, and by using the outside leaves as a parcelling ingredient, you can make all manner of economical dishes.

Serves 6

2 spring cabbages
½ lb (225 g) fat bacon
4 hard-boiled eggs
½ lb (225 g) sausage meat
4 tablespoons soft white breadcrumbs
1 oz (25 g) grated Cheddar cheese
Salt and freshly-ground black pepper
Stock

Remove 6 of the large outer leaves of the cabbages. Carefully cut out the bottom of the stalk from the centre of each leaf. Plunge the leaves into fast-boiling salted water and cook for about 10 minutes until soft and pliable. Cut out the stalk from the cabbage hearts and finely shred the leaves. Cook the cabbage in a little salted water until very tender and drain really well.

Put the bacon through the coarse blades of a mincing machine. Chop the hard-boiled eggs. Combine the cooked cabbage, sausage meat, bacon, breadcrumbs, eggs and cheese, season with salt and pepper and mix well.

Place one-sixth of the stuffing in the centre of each large cabbage leaf and roll up neatly into a parcel (fold in the sides first and then roll up firmly). Tie the parcels with thick cotton so that they do not burst open while cooking. Place the parcels in a lightly-greased saucepan and just cover with some good stock. Bring to the boil and simmer gently for 40 minutes. Strain off the stock and arrange the stuffed leaves on a serving dish.

The stuffed leaves can be served with the stock in which they were cooked, thickened with a little flour and butter mixed together, added to the stock and then stirred until the gravy comes to the boil and is smooth. Alternatively, serve with a home-made tomato sauce.

Cabbage Cooked with Onion and Cream

This recipe makes a change from plain buttered cabbage and is a good accompaniment to a country dish of boiled bacon or a liver and bacon casserole.

Serves 4–6

1 cabbage
1 large onion
2 oz (50 g) butter
4 tablespoons single cream
Salt and freshly-ground black pepper

Discard the coarse outer leaves of the cabbage and the hard stem. Finely shred the cabbage leaves. Peel and finely chop the onion.

Melt the butter in a heavy pan. Add the onion and cook over a low heat until soft and transparent. Add the cabbage and continue to cook over a low heat, shaking the pan to prevent sticking, until the cabbage is just tender. Add the cream, season generously with salt and pepper and toss lightly until hot through.

Brussels Sprouts with Bacon Dripping

The perfect way to cook Brussels sprouts.

Serves 6

2 lb (900 g) Brussels sprouts
2 tablespoons bacon dripping
Salt and freshly-ground black pepper

Remove any coarse outer leaves of the Brussels sprouts, wash them in salted water and score a cross on the cut stalk end. Drop the sprouts into fast-boiling, salted water and cook for about 15 minutes until just tender. Drain well.

Heat the bacon dripping in a heavy pan. Add the sprouts and cook over a medium heat, shaking the pan to prevent browning, for 3 minutes until the fat has been absorbed. Season with pepper and serve at once.

BROCCOLI

In the West Country cauliflowers are almost always referred to as broccoli but in fact the name should, correctly, be used to refer to a variety of large white broccoli which does look very similar to a small cauliflower.

Trevarthan Broccoli or Cauliflower

Serves 4 as a supper or light luncheon dish

1 medium cauliflower or 2 broccoli
1½ oz (40 g) butter
2 tablespoons flour
¼ pint (150 ml) milk
1 egg yolk
¼ pint (150 ml) mint sauce
½ teaspoon orange peel
2½ fl oz (75 ml) orange juice
Salt and freshly-ground black pepper
4 slices white bread
Lard for frying
4 slices ham

Remove the outer leaves of the cauliflower and divide the head into florets. Steam the florets over boiling water until tender but still crisp. Dot with ½ oz (15 g) of butter and keep warm.

Melt the remaining butter in a saucepan. Add the flour and mix well. Gradually blend in the milk, stirring continually until thick and smooth. Very gradually beat in the egg yolk, mint sauce, orange peel and orange juice, cooking until the sauce is the consistency of thick custard. Season with salt and pepper.

Remove the crusts of the bread and fry the slices until crisp in hot lard. Drain bread on kitchen paper.

Top bread slices with a slice of ham and then with cauliflower florets, pour over the sauce and serve at once.

Savoury Curly Kale

Serves 4

1 lb (450 g) curly kale
1 medium onion
1 large cooking apple
3 rashers bacon
1½ oz (40 g) butter
Salt and freshly-ground black pepper
4 eggs

Wash the kale and remove any thick stems. Cook in a little boiling salted water until tender. Drain well and chop with kitchen scissors.

Peel and finely chop the onion. Peel and core the apple and cut into small dice. Remove the bacon rinds and finely chop the rashers.

Melt ¾ oz (20 g) of butter in a heavy frying pan. Add the onion and bacon and cook over a moderately low heat until the onion is soft and golden. Add the kale and apple, season with salt and pepper, mix well, cover with a large saucepan lid and cook over a low heat for 15 minutes, stirring every now and then to prevent sticking.

Fry the eggs in the remaining butter and serve the kale with the eggs on top.

SPINACH

Spinach salads have become a feature of our spring weekend parties. Usually the spinach is up in the garden before the first of the outdoor lettuces and the rather nutty flavour of the leaves makes a good alternative. There are endless variations to this salad theme.

Raw firm button mushrooms, for instance, go well with the spinach; so does crumbled, crisply-fried bacon. Small cooked broad beans are good too and fried, salted earth or pig nuts are fantastic.

Spinach with Triangles of Fried Bread

A Victorian dish with a contrast of smooth spinach tossed in butter and crisp triangles of fried bread.

Serves 4

2½ lb (1·1 kg) freshly-picked spinach
½ teaspoon salt
½ teaspoon sugar
Pinch bicarbonate soda
4 oz (125 g) butter
Freshly-ground black pepper
3 slices thin-cut white bread

Pick over the spinach, discarding any wilted or discoloured leaves and tough stalks. Put 3 pints (1½ litres) of water in a large saucepan with the salt, sugar and bicarbonate of soda. Bring to the boil, put in the spinach, return to the boil and cook for about 12 minutes until the spinach is tender. Drain spinach well (water can be used to make a vegetable stock for soups) and chop roughly with kitchen scissors. Return spinach to a clean pan with 1 oz (25 g) of butter. Season with pepper, toss well, heat through, pile in a serving dish and keep warm.

Remove crusts from the bread and cut each slice into four triangles. Fry the bread triangles in hot melted butter until golden and crisp on both sides. Drain on kitchen paper.

Circle the dish of spinach with the triangles of crisply fried bread.

SAMPHIRE

This dark-green, fleshy plant grows wild in many parts of England, in marshland or coastal areas. It tastes of the sea and is delicious boiled and served with a vinaigrette dressing.

Samphire Penelope

Serve as a first course, as a salad, on pieces of bread as a canapé or as an unusual and delicious sandwich filling.

1 lb (450 g) freshly-gathered samphire
3 tablespoons oil
½ teaspoon made English mustard
1 small clove garlic
1 tablespoon white wine vinegar
Salt and freshly-ground black pepper

Remove any tough stalks and wash the samphire in cold water to remove any sand or earth. Cook in a little boiling water for about 10 minutes or until just tender. Drain really well and chop roughly.

Combine the oil, mustard, garlic (crushed), vinegar and seasoning in a screw-topped jar. Shake to mix well and then pour over the samphire. Chill in a refrigerator before serving.

TOMATOES

The perfect herb to go with tomatoes is basil. Unfortunately it is difficult to grow, and even in the warmer areas of Cornwall tends to be affected by the wind. I have found the best answer is to start it in the greenhouse and then keep pots on the window-sills of the house. According to some it keeps the flies away, but I haven't found it nearly as successful for this function as *eau de Cologne* mint, which seems to keep almost all flies away from the kitchen even in thundery weather which brings them in from the farm in droves.

Tomato Salad

Tomato salads and tomato sandwiches are both delights that I look forward to when the season is in full swing. The salad goes with almost everything and can also be served, by itself, as a first course.

Serves 4

4 very large, ripe tomatoes
4 spring onions
3 basil leaves
3 tablespoons olive oil
$\frac{1}{2}$ teaspoon made English mustard
$\frac{1}{2}$ teaspoon sugar
1 tablespoon white wine vinegar
Salt and freshly-ground black pepper

Scald the tomatoes, remove skins, cut into thin slices and arrange in a shallow serving dish. Chop the white and green part of the spring onions (chipples) and the basil leaves and sprinkle them over the tomatoes.

Combine the olive oil, mustard, sugar and vinegar in a screw-top jar, season well with salt and pepper and shake to mix well. Pour the dressing over the tomatoes and chill in a refrigerator for at least 2 hours before serving.

Layered Tomatoes

The pride of our greenhouses is Geoff's range of tomatoes: mammoths weighing at least half a pound, the ugly Mediterranean variety, small cherry and glowing yellow.

Serves 4

$1\frac{1}{2}$ lb (675 g) potatoes
6 large firm tomatoes
2 bunches spring onions
2 tablespoons parsley
Salt and freshly-ground black pepper
$\frac{1}{4}$ pint (150 ml) stock
3 tablespoons browned breadcrumbs
$\frac{1}{2}$ oz (15 g) butter

Peel and thinly slice potatoes. Dip tomatoes into boiling water, peel off skins and cut into thick slices. Remove the green tops of the spring onions and remove the outer skin of the bulbs.

Arrange a layer of tomatoes in the bottom of a lightly-greased baking dish. Cover with a layer of sliced potatoes, a few spring onions and a little parsley. Season with salt and pepper and continue the layers, finishing with one of tomatoes. Pour over the stock, sprinkle on the breadcrumbs, dot with butter and bake in a moderately hot oven (375° F, Reg 5) for about 45 minutes or until potatoes are tender and the top is crisp and golden brown.

Note: For a more substantial dish the layers can be interspersed with some thin rashers of streaky bacon, or for a more highly-flavoured dish sprinkle the layers with a little dried oregano or finely-chopped fresh basil.

Grilled Large Field or Horse Mushrooms

Serves 4

> 8 large field or horse mushrooms
> 1 large clove garlic
> Salt and freshly-ground black pepper
> Olive oil

Pick over mushrooms and cut off their stems (use these for soup). Remove any grass but do not wash them as this destroys the flavour. Squeeze the garlic through a garlic press.

Arrange the mushrooms, black side up, in a pan, spread a little garlic on each one, season them generously with salt and pepper and brush with olive oil. Grill under a high heat for 3 minutes only and serve at once.

Mushrooms with Mayonnaise

Serves 4

$\frac{1}{2}$ lb (225 g) mushrooms (use only small firm buttons)
2 tablespoons olive oil
Juice $\frac{1}{2}$ lemon
Salt and freshly-ground black pepper
1 tablespoon finely-chopped parsley
$\frac{1}{4}$ pint (150 ml) home-made mayonnaise
$\frac{1}{2}$ teaspoon finely-grated raw onion
1 small clove garlic

Thinly slice the mushrooms. Heat the olive oil in a saucepan, add the mushrooms and cook over a low heat, shaking to prevent browning until most of the oil has been absorbed. Sprinkle over the lemon juice, season with salt and plenty of pepper, remove from the heat, stir in the parsley and leave to cool.

Combine the mayonnaise with the grated onion and the garlic, squeezed through a garlic press. Fold in the mushrooms. Serve chilled.

Note: This goes well with cold meat, poultry or game and can also be served as a first course or as a canapé spread on crisply-fried fingers of fried bread that have been well drained of excess fat on kitchen paper.

Peas with Onion and Bacon

A traditional Cornish dish that works miracles with peas that have gone a little bit too far to be eaten alone.

Serves 4

2 lb (900 g) peas
4 rashers lean bacon
6 spring onions (chipples)
4 lettuce leaves

2 oz (50 g) butter
$\frac{1}{4}$ teaspoon each sugar and salt
Freshly-ground black pepper
$\frac{1}{4}$ pint (150 ml) stock or water
1 tablespoon finely-chopped parsley
$\frac{1}{2}$ tablespoon finely-chopped mint

Shell the peas. Remove the rinds from the bacon and cut the rashers into thin matchstick strips. Trim and chop the spring onions (the green as well as the white part). Roughly chop the lettuce leaves.

Melt the butter in a saucepan. Add the bacon and cook over a low heat for three minutes. Add the spring onions and continue to cook over a low heat, stirring to prevent sticking, for 2 minutes. Add the peas, sugar and salt and shake the pan well. Season with the pepper, add the lettuce leaves, mix lightly and moisten with hot stock or water. Cover tightly and cook over a medium heat for 15 minutes, stirring every now and then, until most of the liquid has been absorbed and the peas are tender.

Mix in the parsley and mint and serve at once.

10

Puddings: Fruit, Plain and Fancy

Dishes that end a meal with pleasure and satisfaction.

Suck Cream

So named because it used to be served with pieces of dry toast which you dipped in the cream and then sucked. Instead of the dry toast try serving the cream with home-made fingers of Cornish Fairings (see page 240) or with charlotte fingers.

Serves 4

2 egg yolks
1 pint (575 ml) single cream
3 tablespoons caster sugar
Grated rind of $\frac{1}{2}$ lemon
3 tablespoons dry white wine

Beat the egg yolks until smooth. Heat the cream with the sugar until the mixture comes to simmering point (do not allow to boil). Gradually pour the hot cream over the egg yolks, beating all the time (this takes three hands, so ask someone to beat while you pour!). Add the lemon peel and wine and pour the mixture into a clean heavy pan. Stir over a very low heat until the mixture thickens like custard and becomes thick enough to coat the back of a wooden spoon. Pour the custard into four glass goblets and chill in a re-frigerator until set and cold through.

Primrose and Marigold Sauce with Ice-cream

Serves 4

1 teaspoon arrowroot
Finely-grated rind and juice of 2 oranges
Finely-grated rind and juice of 1 small lemon
3 tablespoons sugar
2 tablespoons brandy
4 portions Cornish ice-cream

Mix the arrowroot to a smooth paste with a little of the fruit juice. Combine the arrowroot mixture, remaining fruit juice and grated rind in a small saucepan with the sugar. Bring slowly to the boil, stirring all the time and cook for about 3 minutes until the sugar is melted and the sauce has thickened and is quite smooth. Mix in the brandy, taste for sweetness and add more sugar if necessary (the sauce should be a little on the sharp side but not so sharp it will dry your mouth). Remove from the heat and leave to cool for about 10 minutes.

Divide the ice-cream between four dishes, pour over the warm sauce and serve at once.

Thunder and Lightning

There is more than one interpretation of this evocative sounding food. Some say it refers to sandwiches spread with treacle and then with cream. Others that it is open slices of bread spread with clotted cream and then sprinkled with crunchy brown sugar. As far as I am concerned, the pudding is a combination of ice-cream with Golden Syrup poured over it, topped with a generous spoonful of local cream.

Serves 4

1 pint (575 ml) home-made vanilla ice-cream
4 tablespoons Golden Syrup
4 tablespoons Cornish clotted cream

Put two scoops of home-made vanilla ice-cream into 4 glass goblets. Dribble over the Golden Syrup and then top with a dollop of clotted cream. Serve at once.

For a more sophisticated ice-cream, combine the Golden Syrup with a tablespoon of rum, heat gently until they amalgamate and serve as above.

Parson's Dilemma

This Madeira sauce goes so beautifully with ice-cream it is difficult to know whether to drink the last of a good bottle of Madeira or to sacrifice it to the tender mercies of a pudding.

Serves 4

2 teaspoons arrowroot
¾ oz (20 g) butter
¼ pint (150 ml) Madeira
1 tablespoon caster sugar
4 portions Cornish ice-cream

Beat the arrowroot with the butter until smooth. Gradually blend in the Madeira and sugar, beating until smooth. Cook over a low heat, stirring every now and then until the sauce thickens, clears and just comes to the boil. Remove from the heat and leave to cool.

Put the ice-cream into four dishes and pour over the warm sauce. Serve at once.

Hourglass Cream

One of those smooth and simple sweets that slips down gently and makes a cool ending to a meal.

Serves 6

1 oz (25 g) or 2 tablespoons gelatine powder
2 pints (1 litre) fresh milk
2 tablespoons black treacle
¼ pint (150 ml) double cream
2 drops vanilla essence
2 tablespoons caster sugar
Little grated nutmeg

Soften the gelatine in a little of the milk over a slow heat, stirring all the time until dissolved. Add the remaining milk and the treacle and continue to heat until the treacle has melted into the milk – *do not boil*. Pour into a glass bowl, leave to cool and then refrigerate until set and well chilled.

Whip the cream until thick and light. Mix in the vanilla

essence and sugar and spread over the set pudding. Sprinkle a little grated nutmeg on top.

Note: If you don't like nutmeg on puddings substitute coarsely-grated Bourneville chocolate.

Strawberry and Ginger Water Ice

Serves 4

$\frac{3}{4}$ lb (350 g) strawberries
1 oz (25 g) icing sugar
$\frac{1}{4}$ teaspoon ground ginger
Ginger ale
2 egg whites

Set aside $\frac{1}{4}$ lb (125 g) of the strawberries for garnish. Hull and chop the remaining strawberries, mash them with a fork with the icing sugar and ground ginger and purée through a food mill, a fine sieve or in a liquidiser. Put the purée into a measuring jug and add enough ginger ale to measure $\frac{3}{4}$ pint (425 ml). Mix well and turn into an ice cube tray. Cover tightly with foil and freeze in the freezing compartment of a refrigerator or in a deep freeze for about an hour or until the mixture has formed ice crystals to the depth of about $\frac{1}{2}$ in (1 cm) around the sides.

Turn the frozen mixture into a bowl and beat with an electric whisk or rotary beater until smooth. Whip the egg whites until stiff and fold them lightly into the strawberry mixture. Return to the ice cube tray, cover with foil and freeze for a further two or three hours until stiff.

Spoon into glass goblets and decorate with strawberry halves.

Syllabub with Ratifers

'Ratifer' is the West Country rendering of ratafia biscuit, or macaroons.

Serves 6

Rind of 1 orange
$\frac{1}{4}$ pint (150 ml) water
3 oz (75 g) granulated sugar
6 large macaroons
2 tablespoons brandy
$\frac{1}{2}$ pint (275 ml) double cream
Juice of 1 orange and $\frac{1}{2}$ lemon
2 oz (50 g) caster sugar

Cut off any white membrane from the orange peel and cut the peel into very thin strips (and I mean thin!). Combine the water and granulated sugar in a saucepan, bring to the boil, throw in the orange peel and simmer fast for about 30 minutes or until the peel is transparent. Strain off the liquid and leave to cool.

Break up the macaroons, put them in a bowl and pour over the brandy.

Beat the cream until thick and gradually beat in the orange juice, lemon juice and caster sugar. Pile the cream mixture over the macaroons and mix lightly. Divide the mixture between six glass goblets, top with the orange peel and chill before serving.

May Syllabub

Serves 4

Finely-grated rind of 1 lemon
Juice of 1 lemon
1 pint (575 ml) double cream
6 tablespoons runny honey
$\frac{1}{4}$ pint (150 ml) Madeira

1 tablespoon very finely-chopped candied orange or
lemon peel

Combine the lemon rind and juice in a mixing bowl and
gradually blend in the cream and honey. Whisk until
mixture begins to thicken and then blend in the wine.
Continue to whisk until light and thick.

Spoon into individual dishes or glass goblets, sprinkle
over the candied peel and chill in a refrigerator before
serving.

Rum Junket

A perfect dish to serve instead of plain cream with fresh fruit
such as strawberries, raspberries or sliced fresh peaches.

Serves 4

1 pint (575 ml) milk
1 tablespoon caster sugar
1 tablespoon rum
1½ teaspoons rennet
¼ pint (150 ml) double cream
2 teaspoons caster sugar
1 oz (25 g) slivered, blanched almonds
Grated nutmeg

Heat the milk to blood temperature (it should feel neither
hot nor cold). Add 1 tablespoon of caster sugar and the rum
and stir until the sugar is dissolved. Add the rennet, stir
lightly and pour into a glass dish. Leave to set in a cool place
(preferably not a refrigerator) for about four hours until set
firm.

Lightly whip cream until just thick and mix in 2 teaspoons
caster sugar. Roast almonds in a hot oven until golden
brown. Leave to cool.

Spread the whipped cream over the junket, sprinkle with
a little grated nutmeg and top with the almonds.

Apple and Apricot Pie

Serves 6

Pastry:

6 oz (175 g) plain flour
2 teaspoons caster sugar
3 oz (75 g) butter
1 small egg
1 tablespoon iced water

Filling:

8 oz (225 g) dried apricots
10 oz (275 g) granulated sugar
2 tablespoons water
1 lb (450 g) cooking apples
2 tablespoons apricot jam

Cover the apricots with boiling water and leave them to stand overnight. Cook gently in the liquor they were soaking in, with 4 oz (125 g) of sugar, until tender. Drain.

Put the flour into a bowl with two teaspoons of caster sugar. Add the butter and rub it into the flour with the fingertips until the mixture resembles coarse breadcrumbs. Add the egg and water and mix to a stiff dough. Turn on to a floured board and knead lightly until smooth. Chill for 30 minutes then roll out to about $\frac{1}{4}$ in (6 mm) thickness and use to line an 8-in (20-cm) flan case. Line the case with foil, fill with dried beans and bake 'blind' in a moderately hot oven (400° F, Reg 6) for 10 minutes, then remove the beans and foil and continue to cook for a further 10 minutes until crisp and golden brown.

Put the remaining sugar in a heavy frying pan and cook over a moderate heat, without stirring, until the sugar has melted and is the colour of Golden Syrup. Add 2 tablespoons water and mix.

Peel, core and thinly slice the apples. Add them to the

sugar mixture and cook over a low heat, stirring gently, until the apples are transparent. Remove from the heat and leave to cool.

Spread the apricot jam over the bottom of the flan case. Cover with the apples and apricots and pour over the sugar syrup. Chill in a refrigerator until set and serve with cream.

Top Hat

Serves 6–8

12 oz (350 g) self-raising flour
6 oz (175 g) shredded suet
Pinch salt
1½ lb (675 g) cooking apples
2 oz (50 g) raisins
3 oz (75 g) sugar
Pinch cinnamon
Pinch ground ginger
Grated peel and juice of 1 orange

Combine the flour with the suet and a pinch of salt and add enough cold water to make a firm dough. Turn on to a floured board and knead lightly until smooth. Roll out to about ¼ in (6 mm) thick and use two-thirds of the dough to line a 1½-pint (875-ml) pudding basin that has been generously greased with butter.

Peel, core and slice the apples in thick slices. Place the apples in the lined basin with the raisins. Sprinkle over the sugar, spices and orange peel and pour over the orange juice.

Roll out the remaining pastry. Cover the bowl, wetting the edges of the pastry and pressing together firmly. Cover the top with a sheet of well-buttered greaseproof paper and wrap the basin in two layers of foil. Stand in a large pan with water coming one-third of the way up the sides of the basin and steam for 2 hours.

Remove foil and greaseproof paper, turn out and serve with custard or cream.

Apple In and Out

A curious combination of apple and a batter pudding mixture, this makes one of those really delicious 'nursery' type endings to a meal.

Serves 6

4 oz (125 g) flour
½ pint (275 ml) milk
2 small eggs
3 cooking apples
1½ oz (40 g) butter
3 tablespoons soft brown sugar
1½ oz (40 g) lard

Combine the flour, milk and eggs and beat with a rotary or electric whisk until the batter is smooth. Leave to stand for 15–20 minutes.

Peel, core and slice the apples. Melt the butter in a heavy frying pan. Add the apples, sprinkle over the sugar and cook over a low heat, with the pan covered, shaking every now and then to prevent sticking, until the apples are just soft.

Heat the lard in a baking dish until smoking. Add the apple rings and syrup and pour over the batter. Cook in a hot oven (425° F, Reg 7) for 10 minutes then reduce the heat to moderate (350° F, Reg 4) and continue to bake for a further 20 minutes until firm and golden brown.

Note: Due to the addition of the apples the mixture will not rise in the same way as a Yorkshire pudding, but the texture should be light and crisp.

Apples Baked in Nightshirts

Baked apples used to be wrapped in a coating of suet pastry and then boiled. Since the general taste is for less rich and heavy food these days, apples baked in the oven and encased in short pastry seem to be more popular. The pastry casing retains all the flavour of the apples and results in an aromatic, though filling, pudding.

12 oz (350 g) plain flour
Pinch salt
4 oz (125 g) butter
2 oz (50 g) lard
6 cooking apples
3 oz (75 g) sultanas
3 oz (75 g) sugar
Pinch cinnamon and ground nutmeg
3 tablespoons clotted cream

Combine the flour and a pinch of salt in a bowl. Add the butter and lard, cut into small pieces, and rub into the flour until the mixture resembles coarse breadcrumbs. Add enough water to make a firm dough, turn out on to a floured board and knead until smooth. Chill the pastry for 30 minutes before rolling out.

Roll the pastry out thinly and divide into 6 squares large enough to encase each apple.

Peel and core the apples and set each one in the centre of a square of pastry. Fill the cores with sultanas and sprinkle over the sugar mixed with a pinch of cinnamon and nutmeg.

Gather the pastry up over the top, brushing the edges with a little milk so that they will stick and make an airtight package. Place the apples on a greased baking sheet, pastry seam downwards to prevent cracking, and bake in a moderately hot oven (400° F, Reg 6) for 10 minutes, then lower the heat to very moderate (325° F, Reg 3) and continue to cook for a further 20 minutes.

Remove the apples from the oven and put them right way

up on a serving dish. Leave to stand for about five minutes
and then cut a hole in the top of each case. Spoon a little
clotted cream in through the hole and serve at once.

Apple Cribbly

There is something very special about this dish – simple but
different. Originally the recipe would have been served hot
but I find it good cold too.

> *Serves 6*
>
> 4 oz (125 g) caster sugar
> 6 crisp firm eating apples (green Cox's, Granny Smiths,
>   etc., but on no account any soft or floury varieties)
> 3 slices thick-cut bread
> 4 oz (125 g) butter
> Double or clotted cream

Put the sugar into a bowl. Peel, core and cut the apple into
dice. Toss the dice in the sugar until all the sugar has been
used up. Remove the crusts of the bread slices and cut the
bread into cubes about the same size as the apples.

Melt two-thirds of the butter in a heavy frying pan. Add
the apples and cook over a low heat, stirring continually to
prevent sticking until they are transparent throughout and
the sugar has all melted, producing a pale golden juice.
Remove the apples with a slotted spoon.

Add the remainder of the butter to the liquid in the pan
and allow to get very hot indeed. Add the bread and cook
over a high heat, shaking the pan to prevent burning, until
the cubes are crisp and golden brown. Lift out with a
slotted spoon, toss with the apple, pour over any remaining
juice and serve with clotted or double cream.

Note: If the dish is to be served cold, keep the liquid from the
pan separately until just before you serve the dish.

Gooseberry Fool with Elderflower

Freshly-picked elderflowers were once widely used in English country kitchens, to make jellies, wines and to give a delicately lingering flavour of muscat grapes to sweet dishes. They go blissfully well with gooseberries, lifting a plain gooseberry fool from a nursery pudding into something to be savoured and remembered.

Pick the elderflowers when in full bloom, early in the morning before the sun has reached them.

Serves 4

1 lb (450 g) green gooseberries
$\frac{1}{4}$ pint (150 ml) water
2 elderflowers
Caster sugar
$\frac{1}{2}$ pint (275 ml) double cream

Top and tail the gooseberries and put them in a heavy saucepan with $\frac{1}{4}$ pint (150 ml) of water. Add the elderflowers tied in a piece of muslin, bring gently to the boil and simmer slowly for about 20 minutes until the gooseberries are soft. Remove the elderflowers and drain off surplus liquid.

Mash gooseberries with a potato masher and beat in enough sugar to take the tartness from the fruit without making it sickly (the quantity of sugar will depend on the acidity of the fruit). Leave to cool.

Whip the cream until thick and fold it lightly into the gooseberries. Pile into individual glass goblets or into a glass serving dish and chill in a refrigerator for at least 2 hours before serving. The fool should come to the table icy cold.

Gooseberry Charlotte

Serves 4

1$\frac{1}{2}$ lb (675 g) gooseberries
4 tablespoons water

4 oz (125 g) granulated sugar
8 slices thick-cut white bread
2 oz (50 g) butter
1 oz (25 g) brown sugar
½ pint (275 ml) double cream

Combine gooseberries, water and granulated sugar in a heavy saucepan, bring to the boil and simmer for about 20 minutes or until gooseberries are tender. Purée the gooseberries through a fine sieve, a food mill or in a liquidiser and leave to cool.

Remove crusts and finely crumb the bread. Melt the butter, add the crumbs and sugar, remove from the heat and mix well. Whip the cream until thick.

Place a thin layer of crumbs in four glass goblets. Cover with a layer of gooseberries and then a layer of cream. Continue the layers ending with cream on top. Chill well before serving.

Vee's July Fruit Flan

Vee suggested this really delicious fruit flan when we had fresh gooseberries and some frozen redcurrants left over from the last year's crop.

½ lb (225 g) gooseberries
½ lb (225 g) redcurrants
¼ pint (150 ml) water
8 oz (225 g) sugar
2 tablespoons cornflour
8 oz (225 g) plain flour
Pinch salt
2 oz (50 g) butter
2 oz (50 g) lard
1 teaspoon lemon juice
Iced water
2½ fl oz (75 ml) double cream

Combine the gooseberries and redcurrants in a saucepan with the water and sugar. Bring to the boil and simmer for about 20 minutes or until the fruit is tender. Remove from the heat and purée through a food mill or a sieve. Mix the cornflour to a smooth paste with a spoonful or two of the fruit purée. Return the purée to a clean pan, add the cornflour mixture and cook, stirring continually, over a medium-high heat until the purée comes to the boil and is thickened. Remove from the heat and leave to cool but not to set firm.

Put the flour and a pinch of salt into a bowl. Add the fats, cut into small pieces, and rub into the flour with the fingertips until the mixture resembles coarse breadcrumbs. Add the lemon juice and enough iced water to make a firm dough, turn on to a floured board and knead until smooth.

Roll out the pastry to about $\frac{1}{4}$ in (6 mm) thick and line a flan dish (I use one of those attractive white fireproof dishes with a fluted edge that are now on sale in every kitchenware shop). Prick the bottom with a fork, line the pastry with foil and bake in a hot oven (425° F, Reg 7) for 10 minutes, then remove the foil, lower the heat to moderately hot (350° F, Reg 4) and continue to bake for a further 15 minutes or until the flan case is crisp and golden in colour. Leave to cool.

Spread the fruit mixture in the case and chill until set. Top with sweetened whipped cream.

Fresh Peaches with Blackberries

Imported peaches are cheap when blackberries are plentiful along the hedgerows. According to West Country folklore, you shouldn't pick blackberries after the 1st of October, as the Devil spits upon them on that day and from then on they are not fit to eat.

Serves 4

2 large peaches

1 lb (450 g) fresh-picked blackberries
Juice of 1 lemon
Caster sugar
Double or clotted cream

Put the peaches in a bowl, pour over boiling water and leave to stand for 2 minutes. Drain well and slide off the skins. Halve the peaches, remove the stones and put the halves, cut sides up, in four dishes. Cover with the blackberries, sprinkle with lemon juice and a generous quantity of sugar.
Serve chilled with double or clotted cream.

Pears Cooked in Cider

Serves 4

8 small cooking pears
2 oz (50 g) soft brown sugar
2 oz (50 g) sultanas
Pinch nutmeg and cinnamon
Medium dry cider

Peel the pears, leaving them whole with the stalks still on. Place in a saucepan with the sugar, sultanas and spices and pour over just enough cider to cover. Bring to the boil and simmer gently for about 40 minutes or until tender.
Lift out with a slotted spoon. Bring the liquid in the pan back to the boil and keep over a high heat until the liquid is reduced by about half. Pour the liquid, with the sultanas, over the pears and leave to cool. Serve well chilled with cream.

Rhubarb Pudding

Rhubarb is the first fruit of the year to come in the garden, together with the daffodils and the first May blossom. It is one of the most perfect fruits to combine with rich clotted cream. (Rhubarb leaves boiled with water in a stained saucepan will remove even the most stubborn marks from the pan.)

Serves 6

1½ lb (675 g) rhubarb
4 oz (125 g) sugar
¼ pint (150 ml) water
1 scant tablespoon cornflour
½ pint (275 ml) clotted cream

Remove the leaves of the rhubarb, strip off any tough strings from the stalks and roughly chop them. Combine the rhubarb, sugar and water in a saucepan, bring to the boil and simmer gently until the rhubarb is soft and mushy. Strain off about 3 tablespoons of liquid and mix it with the cornflour to make a smooth paste. Add the cornflour to the rhubarb in the pan and continue to cook over a low heat for 3 minutes, stirring continually until the mixture has thickened slightly and is smooth and shiny.

Pour the cooked rhubarb into a glass dish and leave in a refrigerator until chilled through. Dot the top with blobs of clotted cream before serving.

Fruit Roly Poly

Serves 6

8 oz (225 g) plain flour
Pinch salt
4 oz (125 g) suet, shredded
2 peaches
1 cooking apple
6 oz (175 g) blackberries
3 oz (75 g) sugar
Milk or beaten egg

Combine the flour and salt in a bowl. Add the suet, mix well and then add enough water to make a stiff dough. Turn on to a floured board and knead lightly until smooth. Roll out to a rectangle with the pastry about ¼ in (6 mm) thick.

Peel and slice the peaches and apple. Place the blackberries, apple and peaches on the pastry, sprinkle with sugar and roll up neatly like a pancake. Dampen the edges and press firmly together to make an airtight parcel. Brush with milk or egg and bake in a hot oven (425° F, Reg 7) for 5 minutes, then lower the heat to moderate (350° F, Reg 4) and bake for a further 20–25 minutes until the pastry is golden brown.

Serve hot or warm with cream.

Sabina

Serves 4

1 lemon
¼ pint (150 ml) water
4 tablespoons sugar
½ tablespoon ground ginger
3 tablespoons red wine
12 oz (350 g) strawberries
2 ripe bananas

Peel the rind from the lemon with a potato peeler, as thinly as possible and cut into very thin matchstick strips. Squeeze the juice from the lemon. Combine the lemon rind, juice, water, sugar and ginger in a saucepan, bring to the boil and boil hard for 10 minutes, by which time the rind should be soft and transparent. Remove the syrup from the heat, stir in the red wine and leave to get cold.

Halve the strawberries (or cut them into thick slices if they are very large). Peel and thinly slice the bananas. Arrange alternate circles of strawberries and banana in a shallow circular serving dish, pour over the syrup and chill well in a refrigerator before serving.

Somerset Pancakes

The old apple and cheese combination is used here to great advantage as a filling for pancakes.

Serves 4–6

4 oz (125 g) plain flour
Pinch Salt
1 egg
½ pint (275 ml) milk
Olive oil
1 crisp eating apple
6 oz (175 g) cream cheese
2 oz (50 g) clotted cream
Grated rind of 1 lemon
4 oz (125 g) raisins
2 tablespoons caster sugar

Combine the flour and salt in a bowl. Add tne egg and milk and beat with a rotary or electric whisk until the batter is quite smooth. Leave to stand for 30 minutes.

Put ½ teaspoon of olive oil into an omelette pan. Swirl it round and when it is smoking add about 1 tablespoon of batter, tilting the pan so that the batter forms a thin coating across the bottom. Cook the pancake over a high heat until solid and golden brown underneath, then turn it over and continue to cook for a further minute until cooked through. Slide from the pan and repeat the process with the remaining batter. Stack the pancakes one on top of another as they are made.

Peel, core and very thinly slice the apple. Combine the cream cheese with the clotted cream, lemon rind, raisins and apple.

Spread spoonfuls of the cream cheese mixture on the pancakes, roll them up neatly and place in a lightly-buttered baking dish. Heat through in a moderately hot oven (400° F, Reg 6) for about 10 minutes and sprinkle with caster sugar before serving.

Pancakes with Clotted Cream and Blackberries

So simple and yet so absolutely, deliciously British. A special dish for serving in the beginning of September when blackberries are at their best along the hedgerows.

Serves 6

6 oz (175 g) plain flour
Pinch salt
½ tablespoon caster sugar
2 eggs
1 egg yolk
½ pint (275 ml) milk
¼ pint (150 ml) water
1 tablespoon melted butter
Oil for frying
4 oz (125 g) clotted cream
1 lb (450 g) blackberries
2 tablespoons granulated sugar
Juice of ½ lemon

Combine the flour, salt, caster sugar, eggs and egg yolk, milk and water and beat well with a rotary or electric whisk until the mixture is smooth. Leave to stand for 30 minutes and then mix in the melted butter.

Melt about a teaspoon of cooking oil in an omelette pan until smoking. Add a tablespoon of batter, swirl it around the pan over a high heat until the mixture forms a thin, even coat across the bottom and then cook until the pancake is light brown underneath. Turn the pancake over and continue to cook for about 1½ minutes until golden brown on the other side. Slide on to a plate and repeat the process until all the batter has been used, and the pancakes form a pile, one on top of another.

Spread a little cream on to each pancake, cover with blackberries and sprinkle with sugar and lemon juice. Roll up neatly, place in a lightly-buttered baking dish and heat through in a moderately hot oven (400° F, Reg 6) for 5 minutes until just hot through. Serve at once, dredged with a little extra caster sugar.

Avalon Steamed Pudding

Serves 4

Steamed puddings come in many guises and with many flavours. This version uses apples and comes from the Isle of Avalon (such a romantic name) in Somerset.

2 oz (50 g) plain flour
4 oz (125 g) suet
6 oz (175 g) fresh white breadcrumbs
2 oz (50 g) caster sugar
$\frac{1}{2}$ lb (225 g) cooking apples
Grated rind of 1 lemon
Pinch nutmeg
3 eggs

Combine the flour, suet, breadcrumbs and sugar in a bowl. Peel and coarsely grate the apples and add them to the breadcrumb mixture with the lemon rind and nutmeg.

Beat the eggs, add them to the other ingredients and stir well until all the ingredients are mixed. Turn the mixture into a well-buttered pudding dish, cover with a piece of buttered greaseproof paper tied down securely and stand the basin in a large saucepan with enough water to come halfway up the sides. Bring to the boil and simmer for $2\frac{1}{2}$–3 hours, checking every now and then to make sure the water is not evaporating.

Turn out the pudding and serve with warm treacle and single cream.

Butter and Cider Sauce

Serve with steamed puddings.

½ pint (275 ml) cider
3 oz (75 g) butter
Grated peel of 1 lemon
2 teaspoons lemon juice
2 tablespoons caster sugar

Put the cider into a saucepan, bring to the boil and cook over a high heat until it has been reduced by half.

Melt the butter, add the cider, lemon peel, lemon juice and caster sugar and heat until butter is melted and the sugar is dissolved. Simmer for 5 minutes and serve hot.

Devonshire Sauce for Boiled Puddings

A rich, smooth and sweet sauce to serve with almost any boiled puddings.

¼ pint (150 ml) treacle
¼ pint (150 ml) single cream

Put the treacle into a small, heavy saucepan and heat over a low flame until the treacle has melted. Add the cream and continue to cook over a low heat, stirring all the time, until the cream and treacle have amalgamated. Serve hot.

Poor Knights of Maidenwell

Poor Knights are a traditional British pudding and are not at all as poor as they seem; but they are very quickly made and one of the best instant puddings I know. I make mine with sherry rather than the traditional wine and serve them with a raspberry or strawberry jam, thinned with a little lemon juice and water. I have also served them with a marmalade sauce made in the same way and found everyone liked that just as much.

Serves 4

2 eggs
2 tablespoons medium dry sherry
¼ pint (150 ml) milk
4 thick slices white bread
Butter
4 tablespoons raspberry or strawberry jam or marmalade
3 tablespoons water
2 teaspoons lemon juice
Granulated sugar

Beat the eggs with the sherry and milk until smooth. Remove the crusts from the bread and cut each slice into 3 fingers. Melt some butter in a heavy frying pan.

Dip each finger of bread into the egg mixture and fry it in the butter until really crisp and golden brown. Drain on kitchen paper and keep warm while you fry the rest of the pieces.

Combine the jam, water and lemon juice in a saucepan and heat through, stirring continually, until the jam has melted.

Sprinkle the sugar over the bread and serve the fingers with the sauce in a separate dish.

Rice Thunder and Lightning

Serves 4

8 oz (225 g) long-grain rice
8 oz (225 g) clotted cream
4 tablespoons Golden Syrup

Cook the rice in boiling, lightly-salted water until tender but with the grains still separate. Drain well and rinse through with very hot water. Put the rice into four dishes, spoon a quarter of the cream into each dish and mix the cream with the rice. Pour over the Golden Syrup and serve at once.

Note: This is yet another Cornish version of the many 'Thunder and Lightning' dishes.

Cornish Fairings

Soft but crunchy biscuits with a strong ginger flavouring that melt in the mouth.

> 4 oz (125 g) plain flour
> Pinch salt
> 1 teaspoon baking powder
> 1 teaspoon bicarbonate of soda
> 1 teaspoon ground ginger
> ½ teaspoon mixed spice
> 2 oz (50 g) butter or margarine
> 2 oz (50 g) caster sugar
> 3 tablespoons Golden Syrup

Sift the flour into a bowl with the salt, baking powder and bicarbonate of soda. Add the spices and mix well. Rub the butter or margarine into the flour with the fingertips until the mixture resembles coarse breadcrumbs. Mix in the sugar.

Heat the syrup in a saucepan until melted. Add it to the dry ingredients and mix until the mixture forms a stiff dough. Shape into small balls about ¾ in (2 cm) in diameter and place the balls 4 in (10 cm) apart on a well-greased baking sheet. Press the centre of the balls gently with the thumb to flatten them and bake in a hot oven (400° F, Reg 6) for 8 minutes.

Slide from the hot baking sheet on to a cake rack and leave to cool.

11

Cream Teas with all the Trimmings

The West Country is famous for its tea-time glories:
scones with clotted or 'clouted' cream, delicious cakes
and all manner of other specialities.

I HAVE been told that clotted cream first came to the West Country, like saffron, via the Phoenicians who came to Cornwall in search of tin. Clotted cream much resembled a thick, creamy, yoghurt-like substance they had in their own country. Whatever its origin the rich yellow cream of Devon and the slightly thicker, more crusty clotted cream of Cornwall are famous throughout the country.

In the summer most small dairies and many other small shops run a service where the cream can be sent off to anywhere in the country; its keeping powers are good and the thick cream is ideal for spreading on scones to serve with raspberry or strawberry jam at tea time or to spoon over puddings as a rich luxurious topping.

When we first came to Cornwall we couldn't understand why some of the people who worked on the farm insisted on having the more expensive Channel Islands milk instead of ordinary silver top or why, when we shared a cup of tea with them, it had little bubbles of golden fat on the top. Finally I discovered that it was their practice to make clotted cream every day and the milk they had in their tea was the skimmed milk from under the cream which always tasted fine to me.

Devonshire Clotted Cream

2 quarts (2 litres) Channel Island milk or rich, creamy fresh milk

Put the cream into a large enamel bowl that can be put over a flame (or use a flameproof Pyrex dish) and leave it to settle in a cool place for 24 hours until all the cream has risen and settled on the surface.

Put the cream over a *very low heat* and scald until bubbles rise to the surface forming a ring around the top of the pan (this is one of those pieces of cooking magic that it is impossible to describe but you will see the ring, the same size as the bottom of the pan, clearly as it forms.) The length of time this takes depends on the depth of the pan but on no account must the milk be allowed to boil.

Carefully remove the pan from the heat and leave it in a cool place to settle for a further 24 hours.

Use a slotted spoon and carefully skim off the crusty cream from the top of the pan and put it into a bowl. Keep it in a refrigerator until it is required.

Use the buttermilk or skimmed milk from below the cream for baking or for making soups or sauces.

Cornish Clotted Cream

This is sometimes made with whole cream as opposed to creamy milk and the bowl of settled cream or milk is put into a pan of hot water before being scalded. The method takes longer but the cream is thicker and even more rich than the Devonshire product.

A well-heeled and pleasantly eccentric friend of ours brings a large enamel bowl of this solid cream with him on summer picnics (he brings the cream and I bring the food) and a deliciously fattening sight it is.

Teacakes

    1 lb (450 g) plain flour
    Pinch salt
    $\frac{1}{4}$ teaspoon ground cinnamon
    2 oz (50 g) butter
    $\frac{1}{2}$ oz (15 g) fresh yeast
    3 oz (75 g) caster sugar
    3 tablespoons milk
    3 oz (75 g) sultanas

Combine the flour, salt and cinnamon in a bowl. Add the butter, cut into small pieces, and rub into the flour with the fingertips until the mixture resembles coarse breadcrumbs. Cream the yeast with the sugar and add the milk, warmed to blood temperature (neither hot nor cold) and mix until smooth. Leave to stand for 5–10 minutes until the mixture becomes frothy on the top.

Make a well in the centre of the flour mixture, pour in the yeast liquid and mix the flour in from the sides of the bowl to make a stiff dough. Put in a large, lightly-oiled basin, cover with a floured cloth and leave to stand in a warm place for 1 hour.

Remove the dough from the basin, scatter over the sultanas, turn on to a floured board and knead lightly until they are mixed in. Divide the dough into balls about 2 in (5 cm) across, form into flat buns, place on a greased baking sheet and leave to rise in a warm place for 30 minutes. Brush with beaten egg and bake in a hot oven (425° F, Reg 7) for 15 minutes until golden brown.

Serve hot, split in half and spread with butter.

Cornish Splits

These are the authentic vehicles for all that cream and strawberry jam. The splits freeze well. Heat them through in a warm oven before serving. It is important to warm the ingredients before mixing them to ensure a good rise.

> 1 oz (25 g) fresh yeast
> $\frac{1}{2}$ teaspoon sugar
> $\frac{1}{4}$ pint (150 ml) water
> 1 oz (25 g) lard
> $2\frac{1}{2}$ fl oz (75 ml) milk
> 4 oz (125 g) butter
> $1\frac{1}{2}$ lb (675 g) plain strong flour
> 1 teaspoon salt

Cream the yeast with the sugar until smooth. Add the water, warmed to room temperature, and mix in a tablespoon of the flour. Cover with a clean cloth and leave in a warm place, free of draughts, until the mixture is foaming and the yeast working. Combine the lard, milk and butter in a bowl and put into a low oven to warm up to just above blood temperature.

Warm the flour and salt in another bowl to blood temperature. Make a well in the centre and pour in the milk, lard and butter mixture and the yeast mixture. Work with the hands until a smooth dough is formed. Turn on to a floured board and knead lightly for 2 minutes. Put in a large well-buttered basin, cover with a clean floured cloth and leave in a warm place until risen to twice its size.

(It is very difficult to know what twice the size means after leaving the dough for some time. I take the precaution of marking the bowl before covering the dough, at the point to which I feel it should rise.)

Turn out the dough on to a floured board and knead lightly until smooth and elastic. Divide into balls about 1 in (2½ cm) across, press flat to half the height, place on a greased baking sheet, cover again with a floured cloth and leave to rise in a warm place until doubled in size.

Bake the splits in a moderate oven (350° F, Reg 4) for about 25 minutes until golden brown on the top.

Remove from the baking sheet on to a wire rack and rub over with a brush dipped in melted butter, or a piece of buttered paper. Serve in a warmed white damask napkin with the top of the napkin folded over the splits.

The hot splits should be split in half, spread with clotted cream and topped with strawberry jam (preferably the home-made variety with lots of lumpy pieces of strawberries in it). If you buy jam, for this purpose get Tiptree or Elsenham; it is worth having a really good jam.

Cornish Heavy Cake

Everyone I talk to has a different recipe for this scone cake. The following is my version of a Cornish Heavy Cake. It lives up to its name – the inside is delightfully soggy, and served warm from the oven, split in half and spread with butter, it is very good indeed. If you want something quickly made to fill up hungry mouths at tea time you will find this a winner.

> 1 lb (450 g) flour
> Pinch salt
> 2 eggs
> $\frac{3}{4}$ pint (425 ml) cream
> 6 oz (175 g) currants

Sift the flour with the salt into a bowl. Beat one of the eggs with the cream and mix into the flour to form a stiff but pliable dough. Add the currants, mix well and then turn on to a floured board and knead until smooth. Form into a round cake about $\frac{3}{4}$ in (2 cm) thick and place on a baking sheet. Criss-cross the top with diamond shapes, using a sharp knife, and brush all over with the remaining egg, beaten with a little salt.

Bake the cake in a moderately hot oven (375° F, Reg 5) for 30 minutes or until a skewer plunged into the centre comes out clean.

Cool for a little on a wire rack and then cut into slices, split each slice through the centre and spread with butter.

Note: If the Heavy Cake is left overnight, reheat in a warm oven and spread with butter as above.

Rich Devon Cakes

These specialities of Devon are made with clotted cream and therefore extremely rich. They are really more like biscuits than cakes and need no adornment except a dredging of sugar.

Clotted cream, which if you think about it is almost the same in content as butter, replaces any fat in the recipe.

> 1 lb (450 g) plain flour
> $\frac{1}{2}$ lb (225 g) clotted cream

1 egg, beaten
8 oz (225 g) caster sugar

Put the flour into a bowl, add the clotted cream and the beaten egg and mix with the fingertips until the mixture resembles fine breadcrumbs. The mixture should be the consistency of shortcrust pastry and therefore reasonably easy to roll out, but if it is too crumbly bind it with a little milk. Roll out the dough to $\frac{1}{8}$ in (3 mm) thick and cut into circles with a floured 2-in (5-cm) pastry cutter. Dredge circles generously with caster sugar. Place the rounds on greased baking sheets and bake in a moderately hot oven (400° F, Reg 6) for about 15 minutes or until crisp and golden brown.

POTATO CAKES

You find all sorts of potato cakes throughout the West Country. Some are on the savoury side, made with dripping and flavoured with bacon. Others are more suitable for tea time and incorporate currants in the recipe. It was the practice to cook more potatoes than necessary for any meal in order to have some left over to use both for cakes and reheated vegetable dishes.

Honiton Potato Cakes

Serve for tea.

6 oz (175 g) flour
Pinch salt
5 oz (150 g) lard or clear dripping
1 lb (450 g) mashed potatoes
2 oz (50 g) caster sugar
2 oz (50 g) currants
1 small egg, beaten

Combine the flour and salt in a bowl. Add the lard or dripping and rub it in with fingertips until the mixture resembles coarse breadcrumbs. Add the potato, sugar and currants and mix well. Add the egg and mix to a firm dough, adding a little milk if necessary.

Roll out the dough to ¾ in (2 cm) thickness on a floured board and cut into circles 2 in (5 cm) across. Bake the cakes in a moderately hot oven (400° F, Reg 6) for about 10 minutes until cooked through and light golden in colour.

Note: The cakes can also be fried in a little clean dripping or lard until golden on both sides.

Honiton Apple Cakes

>   1 lb (450 g) firm cooking apples
>   1 tablespoon water
>   1 teaspoon cinnamon
>   ¼ lb (125 g) dark brown sugar
>   2 eggs
>   4 oz (125 g) butter
>   2 oz (50 g) currants
>   1 tablespoon finely-grated lemon rind
>   1½ oz (40 g) cornflour
>   4 oz (125 g) fresh fine white breadcrumbs
>   Caster sugar

Peel and core the apples and cut them into chunks. Combine the apples, water, cinnamon and sugar in a saucepan, bring to the boil, cover and simmer until the apples are really soft – about 20 minutes.

Purée the apples through a sieve or a food mill. Separate the eggs and beat the yolks; add the melted butter, currants, apple purée and lemon rind.

Whip the egg whites until stiff and fold in the sifted cornflour (sifting is important with cornflour although it is no longer necessary with plain or self-raising flour). Mix in the breadcrumbs and apple purée mixture as lightly as you can to incorporate them (use a figure of eight movement with a wooden spoon).

Well butter an 8-in (20-cm) cake tin and dredge it with flour. Spoon in the mixture and cook for 40 minutes in a moderate oven (350° F, Reg 4). Leave to cool in the tin, turn out and dredge with a generous amount of caster sugar.

RUM

It is inevitable that with the smuggling trade that went on around the coast of Cornwall and some parts of Devon, rum, always a seafaring drink, was some of the most valuable contraband of the smugglers. Often it was drunk with shrub, a rum liquor flavoured with molasses (apparently the sweetness helped to counteract any taste of sea water in casks of rum that had lain in the sea after a ship had been wrecked). Rum and shrub is a warming drink and still popular in pubs on winter days.

Rum is also used in cooking, usually going into puddings or rich fruit cakes. It is used to flavour junket, too, and to pep up a trifle in the place of sherry. On Christmas Day in the West Country the pudding is often served with a rum instead of a brandy butter.

Rum Butter

3 oz (75 g) softened, unsalted butter
3 oz (75 g) soft brown sugar
Finely-grated rind of ½ orange
3 tablespoons rum
1 teaspoon lemon juice

Cream the butter with the sugar until the mixture is light and fluffy. Add the orange rind and gradually beat in the rum and lemon juice, just a little at a time, beating after each addition until the liquid has emulsified with the butter and sugar mixture. By the end the sauce should have the consistency of whipped cream.

Spiced Rice Puddings

Serves 4

1½ oz (40 g) long-grained rice
1 pint (575 ml) milk
1½ oz (40 g) sugar
2 eggs
2 drops vanilla essence
Pinch ground cinnamon, ginger and nutmeg
4 tablespoons double or clotted cream

Boil the rice in the milk with the sugar for about 30 minutes over a very low heat, stirring to prevent sticking, until the rice is absolutely tender. Remove from the heat and leave to cool.

Beat the eggs until smooth. Add the vanilla essence and spices to the eggs and mix well. Add the cooked rice to the eggs, mix well and spoon into four lightly-greased ramekin dishes. Bake in a slow oven (300° F, Reg 2) for 1½ hours until set.

Pour the cream over the top of the ramekin dishes and serve at once.

Brandy Snaps with Clotted Cream

8 oz (225 g) plain flour
4 oz (125 g) butter
8 oz (225 g) soft brown sugar
2 eggs, beaten
2 teaspoons brandy

Put the flour in a bowl. Add the butter in small pieces and rub into the flour until the mixture resembles fine breadcrumbs. Add the sugar, eggs and brandy and beat with a wire whisk until the mixture is smooth. Well grease a baking sheet. Drop spoonfuls of the mixture, well spaced, on to the sheet and bake in a hot oven (425° F, Reg 7) for about 5 minutes until golden. Remove with a spatula (working as fast as you can), drape over the handle of a wooden spoon, roll up and remove as soon as they become crisp – this will be a matter of seconds. Leave to cool and fill each end with a dollop of clotted cream.

Saffron Yeast Cake

A traditional Cornish cake still to be found on many tea-tables these days, especially in farmhouses, and sold in most bakers'. The cake is more like a bread really and is usually served with the slices spread with butter.

2 tablespoons boiling water
½ small teaspoon strand saffron
1 oz (25 g) fresh yeast
1 teaspoon sugar
¼ pint (150 ml) milk
1 lb (450 g) plain flour
1 teaspoon salt
2 oz (50 g) butter
2 oz (50 g) lard
2 oz (50 g) caster sugar
4 oz (125 g) currants
2 oz (50 g) mixed peel

Pour the boiling water over the saffron and leave it to steep for an hour.

Cream the yeast with the sugar, add the milk (warmed to blood temperature – neither hot nor cold) and mix well. Leave to stand in a warm place until frothing – about 10 minutes.

Put the flour into a bowl with the salt. Add the butter and lard, cut into small pieces, and rub into the flour until the mixture resembles coarse breadcrumbs. Add the caster sugar, currants and mixed peel and mix well. Add the yeast mixture and the strained saffron water and mix to a soft dough. Turn on to a floured board and knead until smooth. Put in a greased bowl, cover with a clean cloth dusted with flour and leave to rise in a warm place until doubled in bulk (about 1 hour). Knock the air out of the dough and put it in a well-greased loaf tin.

Bake in a moderately hot oven (400° F, Reg 6) for 10 minutes, then lower the temperature to moderate (350° F, Reg 4) and continue to cook for a further 30 minutes. Cool in the tin.

Rum Gingerbread

Keep this pale amber ginger cake in a sealed tin or polythene container for three to four days before eating to allow it to absorb moisture and develop its flavour.

>   8 oz (225 g) plain flour
>   Pinch salt
>   ½ teaspoon ground cinnamon
>   1 teaspoon ground ginger
>   3 oz (75 g) butter
>   2 oz (50 g) soft brown sugar
>   2 tablespoons Golden Syrup
>   ¼ pint (150 ml) milk and water
>   1 teaspoon bicarbonate of soda
>   1 oz (25 g) split, blanched almonds
>   2 tablespoons dark rum

Combine the flour, salt, cinnamon and ginger in a bowl and mix well. Combine the butter, sugar, Golden Syrup, milk and water in a saucepan and heat slowly until the butter and sugar has melted. Make a well in the centre of the flour, pour in the liquid and mix well until smooth. Dissolve the bicarbonate of soda in 1 tablespoon of water, pour the mixture into the cake mix and stir really well to incorporate all the ingredients.

Spoon into a well-greased tin about 10 in (25 cm) square

and bake in a very moderate oven (325° F, Reg 3) for 1 hour. Scatter over the almonds and continue to bake for a further 10 minutes. Leave to cool in the tin before turning out.

Turn out, prick all over with a skewer and pour over the rum.

Cider Cake

    8 oz (225 g) plain flour
    Pinch nutmeg
    $\frac{1}{2}$ teaspoon ground ginger
    $\frac{1}{2}$ teaspoon bicarbonate of soda
    4 oz (125 g) butter
    4 oz (125 g) caster sugar
    2 eggs
    $\frac{1}{4}$ pint (150 ml) medium dry cider

Combine the flour in a bowl with the spices and bicarbonate of soda. Mix really well.

Combine the butter and sugar in a bowl and beat until smooth, creamy and light. Beat the eggs and gradually add to the butter mixture, continuing to beat until the ingredients are smooth. Fold in half the flour mixture. Beat the cider until frothy, add it to the mixture, mix lightly and then fold in remaining flour.

Spoon the mixture into a lightly-greased shallow cake tin and bake in a moderately slow oven (325° F, Reg 3) for 45 minutes.

Leave in an airtight tin for at least 24 hours before eating.

Easter Buns

    8 oz (225 g) plain flour
    $\frac{1}{2}$ teaspoon mixed spice
    $\frac{1}{4}$ teaspoon cinnamon
    4 oz (125 g) butter
    4 oz (125 g) caster sugar

2 oz (50 g) currants
2 oz (50 g) chopped, candied peel
1 egg, beaten
2 tablespoons brandy

Put the flour into a bowl with the mixed spice and cinnamon and rub in the butter using the fingertips until the mixture resembles coarse breadcrumbs. Mix in the sugar, currants and candied peel. Mix the egg with the brandy. Add the liquid to the ingredients in the bowl and mix with your hands to a firm dough.

Roll out to $\frac{1}{4}$ in (6 mm) thick on a floured board and cut into 2-in (5-cm) rounds. Place the circles on a greased baking sheet and bake in a moderate oven (350° F, Reg 4) for 20 minutes. Slide on to a rack and leave to cool a little before serving, cut in half and spread with butter.

Scones made with Cream

1 lb (450 g) plain flour
1 teaspoon salt
1$\frac{1}{2}$ teaspoons baking powder
2 oz (50 g) butter
2 eggs
$\frac{1}{4}$ pint (150 ml) single cream
Milk

Sieve the flour into a bowl with the salt and baking powder. Add the butter, cut into small pieces, and rub into the flour with fingertips until the mixture resembles coarse breadcrumbs. Beat the eggs with the cream. Make a well in the centre of the flour and butter mixture, pour in the cream and eggs and mix to a firm dough, adding a little milk if necessary.

Turn the dough on to a floured board and knead lightly until smooth – don't work for longer than is absolutely necessary. Roll out to $\frac{3}{4}$ in (2 cm) thick. Cut into 2-in (5-cm) rounds and bake in a moderately hot oven (400° F, Reg 6) for about 15 minutes until risen and lightly browned.

Serve the scones cut in half with strawberry jam and clotted cream.

Savoury Cheese Scones

These are also delicious to serve with a rich vegetable soup in the winter.

8 oz (225 g) self-raising flour
Pinch salt
Pinch cayenne
6 oz (175 g) grated Cheddar cheese
4 oz (125 g) butter or margarine
1 small egg, beaten

Put the flour in a bowl with the salt and a little cayenne pepper. Add 4 oz (125 g) cheese and the fat, cut into small pieces, and rub into the flour until the mixture resembles coarse breadcrumbs. Add enough water to make a firm pliable dough and knead on a floured board until just smooth. Roll out, using a well-floured rolling pin, to ½ in (1 cm) thick and cut into 2-in (5-cm) circles with a floured pastry cutter.

Brush with beaten egg and sprinkle with remaining grated cheese. Bake in a hot oven (425° F, Reg 7) for about 15 minutes until golden brown. Serve the scones warm.

Somerset Cottage Loaf

Here is my recipe for making your own cottage loaf in the afternoon when all the home-made bread has been sold. It makes one large loaf or two smaller ones.

3 lb (1·4 kg) strong plain flour
2 teaspoons salt

1 teaspoon sugar
2 oz (50 g) fresh yeast
3 tablespoons melted butter or olive oil
1½ pints (875 ml) blood-warm water

Put the flour and salt into a bowl and heat in a low oven until it has reached blood temperature (neither hot nor cold). Cream together the sugar and yeast, add ¼ pint (150 ml) of the warmed water, beat until free from all lumps and leave in a warm place for 5–10 minutes until frothy. Add to the remaining water.

Add the yeast mixture to the flour with the butter or oil and work with the fingers until a smooth dough is formed. Turn on to a floured board and knead until the dough is pliable and elastic. Put into a large greased bowl and cover with a floured cloth. Leave in a warm place until doubled in bulk (see page 245) about 1 hour.

Turn on to a floured board and knead again until all the air has been punched out for about 3 minutes. Pull off two-thirds of the dough and form into a large round. Press flat and top with remaining one-third of the dough, shaped into a circle about one-third of the diameter of the large piece; press down firmly. Push the handle of a wooden spoon well into the loaf and remove.

Place the loaf on a greased baking sheet, cover with a floured cloth and leave to rise in a warm place until doubled in size – about 40 minutes. Brush with milk and bake in a hot oven (450° F, Reg 8) for 40 minutes or until the bottom of the loaf sounds hollow when tapped.

West Country Bread made with Potatoes

This bread is rather on the heavy side but I find it very popular with the men on the farm for 'crib' – elevenses – or tea at the times when they are flat out on sheep shearing, lambing or hay making. It needs to be eaten within 48 hours of being made but will keep well in the deep freeze.

Makes 3 loaves

6 oz (175 g) peeled potatoes
2 oz (50 g) fresh yeast
1 teaspoon caster sugar
1¼ pints (725 ml) water
6 oz (175 g) plain flour
2½ lb (1·1 kg) strong plain flour
2 tablespoons salt

Cook the potatoes in salt water, drain and mash well. Cream yeast until smooth with the sugar, add ¾ pint (425 ml) of water warmed to blood temperature (neither hot nor cold) and mix with the potatoes and 6 oz (175 g) of flour to make a smooth batter. Cover with a clean cloth and leave in a warm place to rise for 1½ hours.

Sift 2½ lb (1·1 kg) of flour with the salt and warm in a low oven to blood temperature. Add ½ pint (275 ml) of water, warmed to blood temperature, and the yeast mixture, and mix with the hands to a smooth dough. Turn on to a floured board and knead for four minutes until smooth and elastic. Cover with a clean floured cloth, put into a lightly-greased or oiled basin and leave to rise for 1½ hours.

Turn the dough on to a floured board and punch down with the knuckles until it returns to a smooth elastic mixture. Divide into three and put into three well-greased 1-lb (450-g) loaf tins. Cover again, leave to rise for ½ hour and then cook in a hot oven (450° F, Reg 8) for about ¾ hour or until the loaf turned out and tapped on the bottom sounds hollow.

Cool on wire racks and leave for at least 4 hours before slicing.

Quick Bread Rolls

These are made with self-raising flour, not with yeast, so they take no time at all to knock up and are very useful in an emergency. They should be eaten as soon as possible and are useful for breakfast, for times when you've forgotten to buy any bread, for a picnic meal or to go with a hearty soup when you want that to fill the family for a completely satisfying meal.

Makes 12 rolls

1 lb (450 g) self-raising flour
¾ teaspoon salt
½ pint (275 ml) milk
Small beaten egg

Combine the flour and salt in a mixing bowl. Add the milk and mix to a firm dough. Turn on to a floured board and knead until smooth but working as little as is necessary to get the dough smooth – overworking will toughen it.

Divide into twelve and shape each one into a sausage-like roll. Brush with beaten egg and bake in a moderately hot oven (400° F, Reg 6) for 30 minutes or until the rolls sound hollow when tapped on the bottom. Serve as soon as possible.

Spiced Cream Cheese

In this recipe the addition of chives and spices to home-made cream cheese, or a commercial brand like St Ivel, makes a delicious sandwich spread, dip or savoury cheese to serve with celery and hot cheese biscuits.

6 oz (175 g) cream cheese
¼ teaspoon paprika pepper
Few drops Worcestershire sauce
2 drops Tabasco sauce
2 tablespoons finely-chopped chives or spring onion tops

Blend the cheese with the paprika, Worcestershire sauce and Tabasco and beat well until blended. Fold in the chopped chives and serve in a small bowl.

An Old English Salad Dressing

In the days of good old 'high teas' salads often featured amongst the many dishes. This traditional dressing is half-way between a mayonnaise and a *vinaigrette* and goes well with summer salads of all kinds. If the dressing is made correctly it should remain thick even if it is stored in a refrigerator for a day or two.

2 yolks hard-boiled eggs
1 teaspoon dry English mustard
Salt and freshly-ground black pepper
3 tablespoons olive oil
$1\frac{1}{2}$ tablespoons white wine or cider vinegar

Put the egg yolks into a mortar and pound with a pestle with the mustard and some salt and pepper until the mixture makes a smooth paste. Gradually blend in the olive oil and vinegar and beat hard with a wooden spoon or wire whisk until the sauce is smooth and thick.

Index

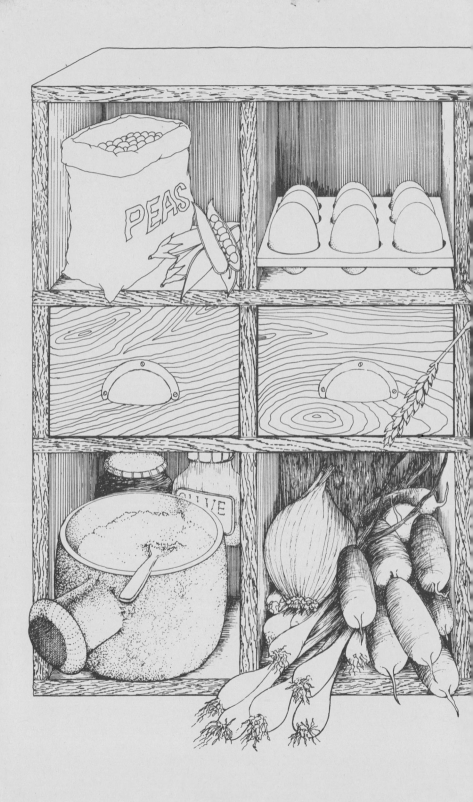